Olive Green English

C1

The authors of film dialogues and vocabulary lists: Wojciech Wojtasiak,
Magdalena Warżała-Wojtasiak

The authors of grammar: Marta Borowiak-Dostatnia (A1-B1), Marcin Mortka (B2-C1)

The authors of interactive dialogues and vocabulary lists: Marta Borowiak-Dostatnia,
Monika Glińska

Proofreading: Monika Glińska, Alicja Jankowiak, Natalia Wajda

Edited by: Alicja Jankowiak

Recordings: Graham Crawford, Joanna Haracz-Lewandowska, Jagoda Lembicz,
Dale Taylor, Marianna Waters-Sobkowiak

Cover design: Marcin Stanisławski

Graphic design and composition: Wioletta Kowalska / Violet Design

Stock photos: © Fotolia.com

Olive Green English C1

Publisher Chung Kyudo

Editors Cho Sangik, Hong Inpyo, Kim Taeyeon, Kwak Bitna

Designers Kim Nakyung, Yoon Hyunjoo, Im Miyoung

First Published December 2017
By Darakwon Bldg., 211, Munbal-ro, Paju-si, Gyeonggi-do 10881, Republic of Korea
Tel. 82-2-736-2031 (Ext. 550-553)

© Copyright SuperMemo World sp. z o.o., 2017
   SuperMemo is the registered trademark by SuperMemo World sp. z o.o.

© Copyright for the South Korean edition by Darakwon, 2017

All rights reserved. No part of this publication may be reproduced, stored in a retrieval system,
or transmitted in any form or by any means, electronic, mechanical, photocopying, or otherwise,
without the prior consent of the copyright owner. Refund after purchase is possible only according
to the company regulations. Contact the above telephone number for any inquiries.
Consumer damages caused by loss, damage, etc. can be compensated according to the consumer
dispute resolution standards announced by the Korea Fair Trade Commission.
An incorrectly collated book will be exchanged.

Price ₩12,000
ISBN: 978-89-277-0955-8 14740
          978-89-277-0950-3 14740 (set)

http://www.darakwon.co.kr
Main Book / Free MP3 Available Online
7 6 5 4 3 2 1   17 18 19 20 21

Table of contents

Introduction **4**

Scene 1 (49): Surgery **8**
Verbs of senses (see, taste, look, feel, smell, hear)
Describing your health and state in emergencies • Giving first aid • Calling an ambulance

Scene 2 (50): Olive wakes up – what now? **16**
Phrasal verbs • Nouns with prepositions • Adjectives with prepositions
Exploring the possibility of business expansion • Maintaining the flow of the conversation • Expressing interest, agreement and support • Presenting your ideas • Persuading

Scene 3 (51): Murray's police interview **24**
Future in the Past
Reporting an accident and a crime • Requesting assistance • Providing information to the police

Scene 4 (52): Beatrice and Murray quarrel **34**
suppose, supposing, say • wish
Stress and the ways to cope with it • The role of patience and perseverance in situations that require waiting

Scene 5 (53): Recruiting Alfie **42**
Mixed conditionals
Highly controversial topics, such as genetically modified food etc. • Getting your point across • Expressing opinions and objections

Scene 6 (54): Murray visits Gennady **50**
Passive forms / Discussing your household budget • Negotiating changes to the budget

Scene 7 (55): What Allen Adams has to say **60**
Verbs followed by -ing, infinitive or both • Verbs with various patterns
Security on the Internet • Local elections • Local volunteer programs

Scene 8 (56): Olive contacts Beatrice **70**
Similes • Compound adjectives
Discussing your business ideas with an investor • Seeking financing for a startup • Presenting your product and business plan • Bringing others to your point of view

Scene 9 (57): Alfie runs away from Russian mafia **78**
It as preparatory subject • It in cleft sentences • It as preparatory object
Registering a company • Contacting the tax office for help • Requesting more details and additional information

Scene 10 (58): Whole truth about Murray **88**
Reported speech: reporting words, orders, suggestions and requests • Reported speech with gerund
Discussing issues relevant to the local community • Managing the funds from the local budget • Discussing controversial topics • Responding to accusations • Challenging the opinions of others

Scene 11 (59): Murray exposed by Beatrice **98**
Inversion in conditional sentences • Inversion with adverbials and in complex sentences • Cleft sentences
Book reviews • Key elements and structure of a good review • Choosing the appropriate register of language

Scene 12 (60): Happy ending? **108**
Participle clauses
Generation gap • Discussing plans for the future between parents and children • Asking for advice • Exploring different courses of development and action

Translation **116**

Introduction

Olive Green is an innovative course for those who want to learn English from the beginning in a way that is both modern and efficient. It is the perfect combination of fun and effective learning of the highest order.

The **Olive Green** multimedia course is based on an **interactive action film**, where you can decide what course the plot will take, as well as play some arcade-type and language games. The course is divided into 12 film scenes for each language skill level.

What is the best way to learn with the Olive Green course?

To begin with, watch the right **film scene** in the multimedia course. We encourage you to watch it several times, so that you can gradually get used to the natural pronunciation you hear and make decisions during interactions. The **subtitles** (available in English and many other languages) will help you understand the content of the dialogue. If you are learning English from scratch, first watch each scene with subtitles in your own language (if available), then with English subtitles, and finally without subtitles. Next, read the **text of the film dialogue** in the book. Then listen to the MP3 recordings of the dialogue, and lastly try to read the text aloud.

Each scene in the book is accompanied by a **list of new words and expressions**. Read them and find them in the dialogue to see how they are used in context, and then listen to the recording of the list.

In the next step, please read the **grammar explanations** describing the most important topics introduced in each film dialogue. You will find many examples of typical applications of all the new structures in these sections.

The multimedia course also includes **interactive dialogues** to let you practice in a variety of communication situations and develop the skills necessary for a conversation in English. Additionally, selected variants of these dialogues have been included in the book, together with the lists of new words and phrases that will help you expand your vocabulary for each topic.

Last but not least, read the **cultural commentary** that will introduce you to some interesting aspects of the culture of the English-speaking countries. The language of the commentaries is simple, but if you are just starting your adventure with English, it may be hard to understand. In that case, please remember that it is always better to try to analyze and understand the general meaning of any English text on your own first – especially if you have been working with the course for some time. Consulting a dictionary for definitions or equivalents of the words that may be new to you should generally be your "second best" option.

To those who wish to continue learning English with **Olive Green**, we recommend the rest part of the course at the other levels.

Enjoy your learning!
The SuperMemo World team
& Darakwon Olive Green team

Olive Green

level C1

Scene 1 (49) Film dialogue and vocabulary

Read the dialogue between Brooks (B) and David (D). Check the list of words and phrases below.

Your pet's suffered some horrible injuries.

B: Look, a lovely entry wound on the shoulder! This must have been messy! Whilst on her back I can feel some spectacular knife scars! Also, a nose job to straighten it after it was savagely broken. Subtle work … Oh vanity! She spared no expense to make it pretty again.

D: She's bleeding to death! Will you get down to treating her?

B: It depends on you. My services come at a price! (…) Lovely! Lovely! For this kind of money, I'll perform the operation and throw in corpse disposal, should the outcome be unsatisfactory!

D: Corpse disposal? Can you save her or not?

B: I can do my best! You must understand that she needs a miracle. Lucky for you, though, I'm one of the few genuine miracle workers around here. Shall we start?

Vocabulary			
pet	애완동물	nose	코
injury	부상	straighten	똑바르게 하다
entry wound	총상	savagely	무자비하게
messy	엉망인	subtle	솜씨 좋은
whilst	~ 동안	vanity	헛됨
spectacular	굉장한, 엄청난	spare no expense	비용을 아끼지 않다
scar	흉터	depend (on)	~에 달려 있다

Olive Green

level C1

Vocabulary				
	service	서비스	outcome	결과
	perform	실행하다	unsatisfactory	만족스럽지 못한
	operation	수술	miracle	기적
	throw in	~을 덤으로 해주다	genuine	진짜의
	corpse	시신	miracle worker	기적을 행하는 사람
	disposal	처리		

What should David do?

D: No! I'm taking her to a real hospital.

Game over. Try again.

D: Do it!

B: All right! I'll need you to assist me, so you must put on a clean apron and thoroughly wash your hands. Don't worry! You'll see your pet fetching frisbees in no time! A word of advice ... I gave her an anaesthetic, but the stuff I use is nowhere near what they have at hospitals. If she starts to scream or struggle, just hold her down and endure it! Okay?

Vocabulary				
	assist	도와주다	anaesthetic	마취제
	put on	입다	be nowhere near	비교가 되지 않는다
	apron	앞치마	scream	비명을 지르다
	thoroughly	철저히	struggle	몸부림치다
	frisbee	원반	hold down	제압하다
	word of advice	한마디의 충고	endure	견디다

Grammar explanations

지각동사 Verbs of senses
e.g. **feel, hear, look, see, smell, taste**

→ 지각동사는 대개 진행형으로 사용되지 않는다.

I **see** a lot of problems up ahead.   앞에 놓인 많은 문제들이 보여요.

I **hear** you are worried.   당신이 걱정하고 있다고 들었어요.

Olive **looks** gorgeous in her new dress, doesn't she?
Olive가 새 드레스를 입으니 정말 멋져 보이는군요, 그렇지 않나요?

I **feel** a bit cold, could you bring me an extra blanket?
약간 추운 것 같군요, 담요를 하나 더 가져다 줄 수 있나요?

It's our favourite brand, their coffee **tastes** like chocolate.
그것은 저희가 가장 좋아하는 브랜드예요, 그들의 커피는 초콜릿 맛이 나죠.

→ 지각동사가 진행형을 취할 경우 의미가 바뀐다.

It's good that I **am seeing** my doctor this week …   이번 주에 의사 선생님을 만나게 되어 좋아요…

Oh no! I **am tasting** my own blood!   오 이런! 제가 제 피를 맛보고 있어요!

The police **will be looking** for us again …!   경찰이 우리를 또 찾을 거예요…!

see

I **see** you've brought your service gun with you. – I perceive that you are armed.
당신이 경찰 총을 가져왔다는 것을 알고 있어요. – 저는 당신이 무장했다는 것을 알아요.

I **am seeing** my doctor this week … – I am meeting my doctor this week.
저는 이번 주에 의사 선생님을 볼 거예요… – 저는 이번 주에 의사 선생님을 만날 거예요.

taste

Their coffee **tastes** like chocolate. – Their coffee has the taste of chocolate.
그들의 커피는 초콜릿 맛이 나요. – 그들의 커피는 초콜릿 맛을 가지고 있어요.

Oh no! I **am tasting** my own blood! – I can detect the taste of my blood.
오 이런! 제가 제 피를 맛보고 있어요! – 저는 제 피 맛을 느낄 수 있어요.

look

Olive **looks** gorgeous in her new dress. – The new dress makes Olive even more attractive than usual.   Olive가 새 드레스를 입으니 아주 멋져 보이네요. – 새 드레스는 Olive를 평소보다 매력적으로 만들어 주어요.

The police **will be looking** for us again …! – They will be searching for us.
경찰이 우리를 또 찾을 거예요…! – 그들이 우리를 찾을 거예요.

feel

I **feel** a bit cold, could you bring me an extra blanket? – I register that the temperature is too low for my comfort.
약간 추운 것 같군요. 담요를 하나 더 가져다 줄 수 있나요? – 온도가 너무 낮아서 아늑하지가 않은 것 같아요.

We **were feeling** the wall to find the door when the lights came up again. – We were touching the wall to find an exit in the dark.   조명이 다시 켜졌을 때 우리는 문을 찾기 위해 벽을 만지고 있었어요. – 우리는 어둠 속에서 출구를 찾기 위해 벽을 더듬거리고 있었어요.

smell

I **smell** fish in the air. – I detect the aroma of food.
공기에서 생선 냄새가 나네요. – 음식 냄새가 나네요.

The cat **is smelling** the fish. – The cat is sniffing the food.
고양이가 생선 냄새를 맡고 있습니다. – 고양이가 음식에 코를 대고 킁킁대고 있습니다.

hear

Suddenly they **heard** police sirens in the distance. – The sound of police sirens was suddenly in the air.   갑자기 그들은 멀리서 경찰 사이렌 소리를 들었습니다. – 경찰 사이렌 소리가 갑자기 공중에서 들렸습니다.

She tried to explain but he just **wasn't hearing** her. – He just couldn't understand her explanations.   그녀가 설명을 하려고 했지만 그는 듣고 있지 않았습니다. – 그는 그녀의 설명을 이해할 수 없었습니다.

➜ 지각동사는 놀라움이나 불신을 나타낼 때 사용될 수도 있다:

It's my song! They are playing my song on the local radio! **Am** I really **hearing** it?
제 노래예요! 지역 라디오 방송이 제 노래를 틀고 있다고요! 제가 제대로 듣고 있는 거죠?

This letter says that I have won some money in a lottery! **Am** I really **seeing** it?
이 편지에는 제가 복권에 당첨되었다고 쓰여 있어요! 제가 제대로 보고 있는 거죠?

➜ 다른 동사들과 달리, 지각동사의 뒤에는 부사가 아닌 형용사가 온다.

He speaks **loudly**. She walks **slowly**. I sigh **wearily**.
그는 큰 소리로 말했습니다. 그녀는 천천히 걸었습니다. 저는 피곤해서 한숨을 쉽니다.

You look **good**! It sounds **great**! It tastes **bad**! It feels **fine**!
당신은 좋아 보이는군요! 멋지게 들려요! 맛이 없어요! 느낌이 좋아요!

Communication situations

Read the following dialogues between two strangers. One of them collapsed in a park.

Excuse me Madam, are you all right?

Dialogue 1

Woman: I don't know. Why am I sitting on the grass?

Man: I assume you must have fainted. Do you feel any pain?

Woman: No, but I can't see you very well and I can barely hear you.

Man: Could you try to look at my finger as it moves?

Woman: I'm sorry. Could you repeat that, please?

Man: Madam, you might have been hit hard on the head. I think we should call the EMS.

Woman: Please do. And could you also inform my son about my condition?

Man: Yes, of course. Where do you have his number?

Woman: There is an ICE number in my phone.

Man: OK. I've got it. I'm calling your son immediately.

---

grass 잔디 | **faint** 기절하다 | **pain** 통증 | **condition** 상태 | **ICE (in case of emergency)** 비상시에는

Dialogue 2

Woman: I'm not sure yet.
Man: Are you able to stand up?
Woman: Oh no, I can't. My leg!
Man: Let me see. Well, it doesn't look nice. Does it hurt?
Woman: When I'm looking at it now, it definitely hurts.
Man: No wonder, it's all covered in blood and bruises. Can you stand on your foot?
Woman: No, it hurts like hell.
Man: Hmm, it might be broken. Let's try to immobilize it until the EMS comes.
Woman: No, don't touch it.
Man: I see. OK, I won't touch it then. Try to stay still while I call an ambulance.

stand up 서 있다 I **hurt like hell** 정말로 아파요 I **immobilize** 움직이지 못하게 하다, 고정시키다 I **EMS (Emergency Medical Service)** 구급대 I **stay still** 움직이지 마세요

Dialogue 3

Woman: Why? Do I look unwell?
Man: Well, you are red all over the face.
Woman: Right. I've been stung by a bee and now I've got an allergic reaction.
Man: And you are swollen. Can you swallow?
Woman: Yes, I've just taken an antihistamine.
Man: Oh, good, so it should start working any moment now.
Woman: Yes. It's not the first time, don't worry.
Man: OK then. Bye.

look unwell 아파 보이다 I **sting** 쏘다, 찌르다 I **bee** 벌 I **allergic reaction** 알레르기 반응 I **swallow** 삼키다 I **antihistamine** 항히스타민제

Vocabulary plus

A&E (Accident and Emergency) 응급실

arm 팔

bandage 붕대

bind 감다

Bloody hell! 빌어먹을!

chest 흉부

compound fracture 복합골절

covered in spots 반점이 생긴

cross the street 길을 건너다

cut 자상, 베인 상처

dislocation 탈구

dizzy 어지러운

dress (상처를) 치료하다

fall down 쓰러지다

first aid 응급 처치

glass 유리

hand 손

heart attack 심장마비

help up 부축하다

ointment 연고

ride a bike 자전거를 타다

rude 무례한

scarf 스카프

shock 충격

shoulder 어깨

sit up 바로 앉다

stick 막대

stitches (수술로 기운) 바늘

strawberry 딸기; 딸기코

sunburn 햇볕으로 입은 화상

suntan 햇볕에 탐

vomit 토하다

Cultural tips

Did you know that ...?

A frisbee (sometimes called a flying disc) is a disc-shaped sporting item that is generally plastic and about 20 to 25 centimetres in diameter. It can be used for recreation and in competitions for throwing and catching, for example, in flying disc games.

Scene 2 (50) Film dialogue and vocabulary

Read the dialogue between Olive (O) and David (D). Check the list of words and phrases below.

Wake up! Wake up, you traitor!

O: You son of a bitch! Do you realize the danger you put me in!

D: Excuse me? I saved your arse back there, didn't I? Well, you saved mine, too, but if I hadn't been there …

O: I only wanted you to bring the documents to me. I'd have dealt with the situation myself!

D: Yeah? How would you have dealt with Murray and his men all by yourself?

O: I'd have figured it out! Maybe blackmailed him … He's hiding something, I know it! If we'd used that information against him … But since you handed the folder over to him… What's that?

D: I took it out from the folder to … I don't know … blackmail Murray if need be?

O: Not bad, Constable Owen. Now we need to find a way to hack this disk!

traitor	배신자	hand over	넘겨주다
realise	인식하다	disk	디스크
save one's arse	~의 목숨을 구하다		

level C1

What should David do?

let Olive do it
C1-02-02

make a suggestion
C1-02-03

D: But I have no idea about these things! (...) Doctor! Help!

Game over.
Try again.

D: Just let me deal with it, okay?
O: What do you intend to do?
D: I know a fellow in London who's got access to all sorts of gadgets and seems pretty tech-savvy!
O: You don't mean ... Oh shit! Not him!
A: David, mate! So glad to see you!

Vocabulary		
	intend	~하려고 생각하다
	fellow	친구
	access	이용하다
	gadget	도구
	tech-savvy	최신기술에 능통한

Grammar explanations

구동사 Phrasal verbs

→ 몇몇 구동사는 목적어를 필요로 하지 않는다. e.g.: *go on, grow up, break down* 이들은 모두 자동사이다:

As the story **goes on**, it gets bloodier and bloodier.
이야기가 진행됨에 따라 점점 더 잔혹해집니다.

Vlad **grew up** as Gennady's errand boy, and later became his hitman.
Vlad는 Gennady의 심부름꾼으로 자랐고 이후에는 그의 살인 청부가 됩니다.

If David's car had **broken down**, Olive would have never got to London.
David의 차가 고장이 났다면 Olive는 결코 런던에 오지 못했을 것입니다.

→ 몇몇 구동사는 뒤에 목적어를 필요로 한다. 이러한 구동사는 타동사이며 분리될 수는 없다:

David was **trying on** a polo shirt which was ridiculed by Olive.
David는 Olive가 놀렸던 폴로 셔츠를 입어보고 있었습니다.

Sergey was not pleased at all when his dad told him to **look after** Vlad.
그의 아버지가 Vlad를 돌보라고 말했을 때 Sergey는 전혀 기쁘지 않았습니다.

Yuri **put out** the cigarette and left Gennady's office.
Yuri는 담뱃불을 끄고 Gennady의 사무실을 떠났습니다.

When Vlad ate all the crisps, he **threw away** the empty bag.
Vlad는 감자칩을 다 먹고 빈 봉지를 버렸습니다.

→ 몇몇 구동사의 경우 목적어가 가운데에 위치할 수 있다. 이러한 구동사는 타동사이며 분리될 수 있다:

Yuri **put out** the cigarette and left Gennady's office. → Yuri **put** the cigarette **out** and left Gennady's office.
Yuri는 담뱃불을 끄고 Gennady의 사무실을 떠났습니다.

When Vlad ate all the crisps, he **threw away** the empty bag. → When Vlad ate all the crisps, he **threw** the empty bag **away**.
Vlad는 감자칩을 다 먹고 빈 봉지를 버렸습니다.

→ 목적어가 대명사일 경우 (*it, me, him* etc.), 목적어는 구동사의 가운데에 위치해야만 한다:

Sergey was Vlad's guide and had to **show** him **around**.
Sergey는 Vlad의 가이드여서 그에게 주변을 안내해 주어야 했습니다.

명사와 전치사
Nouns with prepositions

→ 몇몇 명사는 특정한 전치사를 필요로 한다:

complaint prejudice	against
affection hatred reason respect search	for
break	from
pride	in
neglect victim	of
control	over
damage disgrace objection reaction	to

형용사와 전치사
Adjectives with prepositions

→ 몇몇 형용사는 특정한 전치사를 필요로 한다:

excited	about
good	at
responsible	for
different	from
fluent	in
scared typical	of
hooked keen	on
addicted attracted similar	to
bored disgusted obsessed pleased	with

Remember!

몇몇 형용사는 의미에 따라 두 개의 전치사를 취하기도 한다.

Gennady wasn't really **angry with** his men **about** the mess in the hotel.
(사람에게 화가 난 경우 / 상황에 화가 나는 경우)

He said to Murray on the next day: "It was so **kind of** you to cover all the damage in the hotel. You have always been so **kind to me**!"

→ *it's kind / nice of Murray* – Murray의 친절한 행위에 대해 감사하는 경우
→ *Murray is kind / nice to Gennady* – Murray가 Gennady에게 친절하게 대한다는 것을 알고 있을 경우

Communication situations

Read the following dialogues. Gennady and another gangster are talking about their business plans.

Good morning, everyone.

Dialogue 1

Gangster: Good morning, Gennady, and thanks for joining us. Would you like something to drink?

Gennady: Coffee would be fine. Now, let's get down to business.

Gangster: As you are aware, we have to expand our business.

Gennady: Yes, I know what you mean. Personally, I'd go for something legal. We should focus on the real estate market.

Gangster: Great minds think alike.

Gennady: What appears to be a problem is the mortgage policy. After the financial crisis banks are no longer as generous as they used to be. We should find another way of financing the purchase.

Gangster: Leave it with me.

Gennady: OK. Fine.

---

expand 확장시키다 | **real estate market** 부동산 시장 | **Great minds think alike.** 훌륭한 사람들은 생각이 같다. | **mortgage** 담보 대출 | **generous** 관대한 | **finance** 자금을 조달하다

Dialogue 2

Gangster: You seem to be upset.

Gennady: Yes, I am. But never mind. Carry on, please.

Gangster: The main reason for this meeting is the fact that we need to start thinking about entering new markets.

Gennady: Could you be more precise? Do you mean domestic or international?

Gangster: Let us consider the domestic market.

Gennady: Yes, I know what you mean. Personally, I'd go for something legal. We should focus on the real estate market.

Gangster: I am not so sure.

Gennady: Why not? What's wrong with this market? It's been pretty stable for years, it's safe and the money is good. Piece of cake, I'd say.

Gangster: How about consulting the headquarters in Moscow? Won't they have something to say about it?

Gennady: You've got a point. I'll get in touch with them today. No time like the present.

Gangster: Keep me updated, please.

---

consult 상담하다 l **headquarters** 본사 l **No time like the present.** 지금이 적기이다. l **keep updated** 최신 소식을 계속해서 전하다

Dialogue 3

Gangster: Generally speaking, I want to expand the business all over.

Gennady: So if I understand you correctly, you want to go international.

Gangster: That's exactly what I mean.

Gennady: Keep talking.

Gangster: I thought of the real estate market – a legal business for a change. I've already had some research done.

Gennady: Sounds promising. Let me have a look at those figures.

---

all over 모든 곳에, 전체에 l **keep talking** 계속 얘기하세요 l **for a change** 여느 때와 달리 l **figures** 수치

Dialogue 4

Gangster: So where does it lead us?

Gennady: Well, we could build up a portfolio of properties and rent them, instead of just buying and selling.

Gangster: Southern Europe is the best holiday destination.

Gennady: What's wrong with you, man? Is that a joke?

---

property 재산, 소유물 | **holiday destination** 휴양지

Vocabulary plus

look into ~을 조사하다

penetrate 간파하다; 관통하다

There is still some ground to cover. 여전히 갈 길이 멀다.

think over ~을 심사숙고하다

Cultural tips

Did you know that …?

In English, there are several useful idioms with the word "time":

There is no time like the present. (used for saying that someone should do something now, and not wait until later)

Time is money. (used for saying that time is a valuable commodity, and that you should put it to good use, otherwise you'll lose more than you gain)

It's time for a change. (used for saying that it's high time you stopped what you are doing and started doing something different with your life)

It's a waste of time. (used for saying that something is a useless and pointless way to spend your time)

Scene 3 (51) — Film dialogue and vocabulary

Read the dialogue between Murray (M) and a policeman (P). Check the list of words and phrases below.

P: Of course, I'm not authorised to share any details with you since the investigation is in progress, but it seems your employees were involved in some criminal activity. A sizeable amount of narcotics was found in the warehouse!

M: Drugs?

P: Yes. Mr Murray, were you not aware of the fact that some of your security personnel had very impressive criminal records? You must have run a check on them before you took them on?

M: Well, no, I didn't. They were recommended to me by a friend of mine. He spoke highly of their qualifications, so I took his word for it. It seems I should not have be so gullible, should I?

P: Did you ever see any of them using drugs?

M: Yes, in fact, I made a formal complaint about it to Josh who ran the team.

P: That would be Joshua Alden?

M: Yes! As I said, I made a complaint to him because it reached my ears that his people and himself had been seen smoking marijuana on duty. Most likely, I would have fired them very soon in any case.

level **C1**

> I see. ... Do you know a man named Martin Willis? 50 years of age. A private investor from London.

Vocabulary

of course	물론	
be authorised	권한이 있다	
detail	세부 사항	
investigation (into)	조사	
be in progress	진행 중이다	
criminal activity	범죄 행위	
sizeable	꽤 많은	
amount	양	
narcotic	마약	
warehouse	창고	
be aware	~을 알다	
personnel	(조직의) 인원	
criminal record	전과 기록	
run checks (on)	~을 조사하다	
take on	고용하다	
recommend	추천하다	
qualifications	자격	
gullible	남을 잘 믿는	
drug	마약	
make a complaint	항의하다	
reach one's ears	귀에 들어오다	
marijuana	마리화나	
on duty	근무 중인	
most likely	아마, 필시	
fire	해고하다	
in any case	어쨌든	
named	~라고 불리는	
private investor	개인 투자가	

level C1 Scene 3 (51)

What should Murray do?

M: Yes, I do! Willis ... well ... He was romantically involved with my wife years ago. He never got over their breakup. Why do you mention him?

P: Strangely enough, his body was found in the warehouse, too. In his wallet we found a photo of your wife. There's a possibility that he and your security guards were conspiring against you. We'll certainly need to look into that as well! Thank you for the conversation.

Vocabulary				
	be romantically involved (with)	~와 사랑하는 사이이다	possibility	가능성
	breakup	이별	security guard	보안 요원
	mention	언급하다	conspire (against)	음모를 꾸미다
	Strangely enough ...	이상하게도		

level C1

M: No, I'm afraid I don't know a Martin Willis.

P: That's strange, because we've got reasons to believe he knew your wife intimately and ook a keen interest in you, too. Mr Murray, we'll need to meet again very soon.

| strange | 이상한 | take keen interest in | 상당한 관심을 갖다 |
| know intimately | 속속들이 알고 있다 | | |

What's happened to Martin Willis?

Grammar explanations

과거상에서의 미래 Future in the Past

과거상에서의 미래는 간접 화법에서 상당히 자주 사용되며, 조동사가 과거형으로 변경된다. 과거상에서의 미래는 과거 시점에서 미래에 대한 문장을 만들 때 사용된다.

> will → would

Beatrice: This crappy trip **will not change** a thing!
Beatrice: 이런 형편없는 여행은 아무것도 바꿔 놓을 수 없을 거예요!

Beatrice said to Martin that the crappy trip **wouldn't change** a thing.
Beatrice는 Martin에게 형편없는 여행은 아무것도 바꿔 놓을 수 없을 것이라고 말했습니다.

> be going to → was/were going to

Martin Willis: I **am not going to** kill anybody.
Martin Willis: 저는 아무도 죽이지 않을 거예요.

Martin Willis said that he **wasn't going to** kill anybody.
Martin Willis는 아무도 죽이지 않겠다고 말했습니다.

> Present Continuous → Past Continuous

David: After this conversation, I **am calling** my sergeant to tell him everything about you.
David: 대화가 끝난 후 저는 경사에게 전화를 걸어 당신에 관한 모든 것을 그에게 이야기하겠어요.

David told Murray that after the conversation he **was calling** his sergeant.
David는 대화가 끝난 후 경사에게 전화를 걸겠다고 Murray에게 말했습니다.

과거상에서의 미래(would + 부정사)는 현재나 미래에 대해 가정하는 서술을 하기 위한 가정법 문장에서도 사용된다.

Vlad: Would I look like a Brit in a shirt like this? ← Vlad is making a **hypothesis** about **the present**. Vlad: 이러한 셔츠를 입으면 제가 영국인처럼 보일까요? ← Vlad는 현재에 대해 가정하고 있다.

과거상에서의 미래완료(would + have + 과거분사)는 과거에 대해 가정하는 서술을 하기 위한 가정법 과거완료 문장에서도 사용된다.

Murray: I would have fired them very soon in any case. ← Murray is making a **hypothesis** about **the past**.
Murray: 어떤 경우라도 그들을 곧바로 해고했을 것입니다. ← Murray는 과거에 대해 가정하고 있다.

Olive wouldn't have managed to follow her mysterious employer's new orders. There was no time! → She didn't follow the new orders. Olive는 비밀에 싸인 고용주의 새로운 명령을 따르지 않았을 거예요. 시간이 없었어요! → 그녀는 새로운 명령을 따르지 않았습니다.

> **Remember!**
> 과거상에서의 미래는 발생하지 않았거나 발생하지 않았을 행동, 또는 완료되지 않은 상태의 행동을 설명할 때 사용된다.

She wouldn't have wanted to hurt Curtis. She never hurts people if she can help it! → She didn't want to hurt Curtis and she did not hurt him. 그녀는 Curtis를 다치게 하고 싶지 않았을 거예요. 그녀는 될 수 있다면 누구도 다치게 하지 않아요! → 그녀는 Curtis를 다치게 하고 싶지 않아서 그를 다치게 하지 않았습니다.

She would probably have tackled Murray herself – she's a good fighter. → But she didn't tackle him and we'll never know how that would have gone. 그녀는 아마 자신이 직접 Murray를 상대했을 거예요 – 그녀는 싸움을 잘 하거든요. → 하지만 그녀는 그와 상대하지 않았고 그런 일이 벌어졌으면 어떻게 되었을지는 결코 알 수 없습니다.

과거상에서의 미래가 현재까지도 계속해서 영향을 미치고 있는 문장에서 사용될 때에는 시제의 변화가 일어나지 않는다 (조동사의 시제가 변화하지 않는다). 비교:

Beatrice said: My life with Robert will never be easy. Beatrice는 말했습니다: Robert와 함께하는 인생은 결코 순탄하지 않을 거예요.

Beatrice realised (probably years ago) that her life with Robert would never be easy.
→ That life/relationship is over. Beatrice는 Robert와 함께하는 인생이 결코 순탄하지 않을 것이라는 점을 (아마 몇 년 전에) 깨달았습니다. → 그러한 인생/관계는 끝났습니다.

하지만:

David said: My life with Olive will never be easy. David는 말했습니다: Olive와 함께하는 인생은 결코 순탄하지 않을 거예요.

David realised (a couple of days earlier) that his life with Olive will never be easy.
→ This life/relationship is ongoing. David는 Olive와 함께하는 인생이 결코 순탄하지 않을 것이라는 점을 (이틀 전에) 깨달았습니다. → 그러한 인생/관계는 계속되고 있습니다.

Communication situations

Read the following dialogues between a police officer and a caller who needs help.

Good evening, London Police Station, officer Johnson, how may I help you?

Dialogue 1

Caller: I'm calling to report a car collision.

Officer: Do you need an ambulance or fire service?

Caller: Yes. Four vehicles have collided and somebody might be injured.

Officer: All right. What's your location?

Caller: I was first on M25, then A225, and now I have taken the exit to Dartford.

Officer: OK. We have already got this entry in our system. The emergency services are on their way. Does somebody in your car or you personally need help?

Caller: If the rescue takes hours, a hot drink may be needed.

Officer: OK. Before I take your details, are there any children in the car?

Caller: Yes, two. A 1-year-old and a 7-year-old.

Officer: Does the baby need a bottle or is it breast-fed?

Caller: Depending on the time. In 5 hours she will need a bottle.

Officer: OK. I've got it. Let me take your details now.

---

fire service 소방대 I **injured** 다친 I **location** 위치 I **exit** 출구 I **breast-fed** 모유를 먹이는

Dialogue 2

Caller: I'm calling to report arson.
Officer: Are you a witness or a victim of the arson?
Caller: Well, I'm fine but the fire has affected my property.
Officer: OK. What has been affected?
Caller: My car.
Officer: All right. When did it take place?
Caller: I don't know. I've been away since Tuesday.
Officer: OK. Police officers are on their way. May I take your details?

---

arson 방화 | **witness** 목격자 | **victim** 피해자

Dialogue 3

Caller: I'm calling to report a car collision.
Officer: Do you need an ambulance or fire service?
Caller: I'm fine but I think the other driver is bleeding.
Officer: All right, the ambulance in on its way. Can you give me some details of the collision? How many vehicles are involved?
Caller: Two: a truck and my car.
Officer: OK. Where has the collision taken place?
Caller: We are 50 metres from Canary Wharf Station.
Officer: I see. Has your collision blocked the traffic in any way?
Caller: Yes, unfortunately we have blocked the whole crossing.
Officer: OK. Please stay in your car and wait for the police officer.

---

be involved 연관되다

Vocabulary plus

breakdown service 고장 수리 서비스

casually 격식을 차리지 않고

dustbin 쓰레기통

fencing 울타리

fire brigade 소방서; 소방대

garden 정원

hard to say 말하기 어려운

instruct 지시하다

later on 나중에

looting 약탈

neighbourhood 지역

outskirts 교외

passenger car 승용차

pile-up 연쇄 추돌

shed 작업장

smashed 완전히 부서진

smell 냄새를 맡다

step out of ~에서 나오다

subject of the event 사건의 대상

terrace 테라스

track down ~을 찾아내다

traffic ban 교통 통행 금지

vandalism 공공 기물 파손죄

zebra crossing 횡단보도

Cultural tips

Did you know that ...?

There are different names in English for a road designed to allow traffic to safely travel at fast speeds:
+ motorway (in the United Kingdom and Ireland)
+ freeway (in Australia and parts of the United States and Canada)
+ expressway (some parts of Canada, parts of the United States, and many Asian countries)

The **M25 motorway** (188 kilometres long) is one of the world's longest orbital roads that encircles almost all of Greater London in the UK.

Scene 4 (52) — Film dialogue and vocabulary

Read the dialogue between Beatrice (B) and Murray (M). Check the list of words below.

Found dead? With Josh? And other security men?

B: Did you have him killed?
M: That's preposterous! I have no idea who did him in!
B: You did!

| preposterous | 터무니없는 |

level C1

What should Murray do?

M: Is it one of your "weird days", Beatrice? You couldn't resist just one more pill, could you? I did not kill that maniac! And I wish you'd stop blaming me for everything – especially how shitty your life is! Now get out of my sight!

(…) Police? This is Beatrice Murray, resident of Campbell Manor in Old Berry. There are things you should know about my husband … Robert Murray.

Game over. Try again.

Vocabulary		
	resist	참다, 견디다
	pill	약
	maniac	미치광이
	shitty	엉망진창인
	get out of sight	내 앞에서 사라져!

M: I didn't! Look, this obsessive maniac has been meddling with our life for years! Plotting to bring us down, purchasing data from people we trusted, digging out filth he could use against us ...

B: And he could have found plenty of it, couldn't he?

M: What?

B: Filth ... There's so much of it in this house. Suppose he revealed your affairs ... But it wouldn't have worked, would it? Maybe hurt your reputation a little bit, but nothing to lose sleep over! But say he brought to people's attention the transactions you handle ... Not the ones you boast about in public ... I mean the ones where the really big money is involved. The ones you conclude with big, scary men with cold eyes, speaking with foreign accents. I wonder ... I wonder if they are something the police would take interest in.

M: Empty words, Beatrice. You talk so much but do so little. That's the real reason why your life's been shitty!

Vocabulary

obsessive	집요한	lose sleep over	잠도 못 자고 ~을 걱정하다
maniac	미치광이	bring to one's attention	~의 관심을 끌다
meddle (with)	~에 관여하다	handle	처리하다
purchase	구매하다	boast (about)	~에 대해 자랑하다
dig out	~을 파내다	in public	공공연하게
filth	도덕적 부패, 비리	scary	무서운
plenty of	많은	foreign accent	외국 말투
suppose	추정하다	wonder	궁금하다
reveal	폭로하다	empty words	무의미한 말
hurt one's reputation	명성에 해를 끼치다	shitty	엉망진창인

Grammar explanations

Suppose/Supposing/Say

suppose/supposing/say:
- ➔ 가정법 의문의 맨 앞에서 사용된다.
- ➔ 가능한 상황을 (또한 그 결과를) 예상할 때 사용된다.
- ➔ 구체적인 설명은 아래와 같다:

현재 → 언젠가 일어날 수 있는 일에 대해 언급할 때 사용된다:

Suppose he **doesn't rescue** Olive ... What then?
그가 Olive를 구조하지 못한다면… 어떻게 될까요?

과거 → 가능성을 고려하거나 일어날 가능성이 낮은 일을 언급할 때 사용된다:

Say I **had** an idea how to read what's on the floppy disc, what would you do?
플로피 디스크에 무엇이 들어 있는지 알 수 있는 방법이 내게 있다면 어떻게 하시겠어요?

과거완료 → 과거에 일어났을 수 있는 사건을 설명할 때 사용된다:

Supposing Murray **had** erased all the data from the floppy disc?
Murray가 플로피 디스크에 있는 모든 데이터를 지웠다고 가정하면요?

Wish

Wish 구조는 주로 현재나 과거에 대한 후회를 표현한다.
하지만 아래와 같은 것들도 표현할 수 있다:

- ➔ 행위에 대한 비난/불승인: 주어 + *wish* + 사람 + *would* + 부정사

    I wish you wouldn't ask the same question all the time! ➔ I've heard your question so many times that I can't stand it anymore.
    당신이 항상 똑같은 질문을 하지 않았으면 좋겠어요! → 저는 당신의 질문을 너무 여러 번 들어서 더 이상 견딜 수가 없어요.

- ➔ 능력에 대한 유감: 주어 + *wish* + 사람 + *could* + 부정사

    He wishes he could speak English without any difficulties. ➔ He can't and he feels sorry about it.
    그는 어려움 없이 영어를 구사할 수 있기를 바라요. → 그는 그럴 수 없어서 그에 대해 안타까움을 느껴요.

- ➔ 행동에 대한 유감: 주어 + *wish* + 사람 + 과거진행형

    We wish we were doing something more interesting. ➔ What we are currently doing is boring.
    우리는 보다 흥미로운 일을 했으면 해요. → 현재 우리가 하고 있는 일은 지루해요.

Communication situations

Read the following dialogue between two podcasters discussing the subject of waiting.

Hello and welcome to our weekly podcast on personal development. Today we are going to talk about dealing with different kinds of waiting we encounter in our daily lives.

Dialogue 1

Guest: Especially when we're forced to wait in very difficult circumstances.

Host: Precisely. And those who suffer are often left without real support. People just keep telling them to "stay positive".

Guest: Well, the crux of the matter is that "positive" doesn't necessarily equal "happy" or "pleasant".

Host: Precisely. I think most psychologists, religious authorities and parents would agree that growth is painful.

Guest: Absolutely. We even talk about "growing pains", don't we?

Host: Right. So we shouldn't fear pain and change. But what constructive strategies can we develop to cope with them better?

Guest: One of the healthy ways of dealing with it would be embracing all the waiting we're forced to endure.

Host: What exactly do you mean? Can we find any examples of behaviours that could help us in such circumstances?

Guest: Well, when we are hurting and confused, we usually need answers.

Host: I imagine that would involve formulating the questions first.

Guest: Yes and no. Some questions tend to be more useful than others.

Host: What do you mean? What do you recommend we ask ourselves then?

Guest: We may as well ask "why not me". But the really good question is, "What can I learn from it?".

Host: So, we can either torment ourselves or concentrate on the bigger picture. Both options are painful, but the latter seems more productive in the long run.

---

crux of the matter 가장 중요한 점 | **religious authorities** 종교 단체 | **growing pains** 성장통 | **constructive** 건설적인 | **hurting and confused** 괴롭고 혼란스러운 | **learn** 배우다 | **torment** 고통, 고뇌 | **bigger picture** 더 큰 그림 | **latter** 후자

Vocabulary plus

absolute 절대적인

act 행동하다

annoying 짜증스러운

big break 결정적인 기회

burden 짐, 부담

careful attention 유념

catch unawares 놀라게 하다

commute 출퇴근

daily life 일상 생활

dough 돈

duration 기간

effective strategy 효과적인 전략

embrace 수용하다

encounter 맞닥뜨리다

Every cloud has a silver lining. 고생 끝에 낙이 온다.

force 힘

God 신

group therapy 집단 요법

health 건강

hide one's head in the sand 현실을 외면하다

impatient 참을성이 없는

in jeopardy 위기에 처한

in return ~에 대한 반응으로

in time of need 필요할 때

intolerable 견딜 수 없는

keep in touch with 연락을 취하다

malady 심각한 문제

mind over matter 정신력에 달린 문제

misery 고통

moan 불평하다

network 망, 관계

no pain, no gain 고통 없이 얻는 건 없다

not to let oneself realize 깨닫지 못하게 하다

nowadays 요즈음에

overlook 간과하다

perception 인식

personal development 개인적인 발전

realisation 자각, 인식

reject 거절하다

release 풀어 주다

similar 유사한

sizeable portion 상당 부분

source 근원, 원천

state 상태

supernatural 초자연적인

support 지지

support group 협력 단체

terminology 전문 용어

there's no escaping 어쩔 수 없다

try somebody's patience 인내심을 시험하다

unconsciously 무의식적으로

understanding 이해심

virtually endless 사실상 끝없는

waiting 대기

waiting room 대기실

war 전쟁

wasted 헛된

weekly 매주의

Cultural tips

Did you know that …?

Carpooling, a more and more popular way of commuting, is the sharing of car journeys so that more than one person travels in a car. Authorities often encourage carpooling, especially during periods of high pollution or high fuel prices.

Scene 5 (53)   Film dialogue and vocabulary

Read the dialogue between Alfie (A) and Olive (O). Check the list of words and phrases below.

My poor girl, what have you gotten yourself into? Shooting people has never been your cup of tea.

We need your help!

A: Of course you do! I knew it would come to this the moment I set eyes on that guy. Such a bad influence on you! If he hadn't replaced me at your side, you wouldn't be in that miserable condition now!

O: You've never been at my side. More like in the general proximity of my wallet.

A: How can you even say that? The special bond between us went beyond money! All right! What's the job and how much are you offering?

D: We're not paying you! You're just doing it!

A: Like hell I am!

Vocabulary

get oneself into	어떤 상황에 빠지다	at one's side	~의 곁에
be one's cup of tea	~의 취향이다	general	일반적인
set one's eyes on	눈독을 들이다	in the proximity of	~의 근처에
influence (on)	영향을 주다	go beyond	~을 초과하다
replace	대신하다	offer	제안하다

Olive Green

What should David do?

D: Olive, I think he needs some time to think about it! Why don't I take him back to the shed for a few more days?

A: By all means! I adore eating rotten food and sleeping next to an overflowing bucket of faecal matter. And as for the company of the French ... Magnifique! Can we go already?

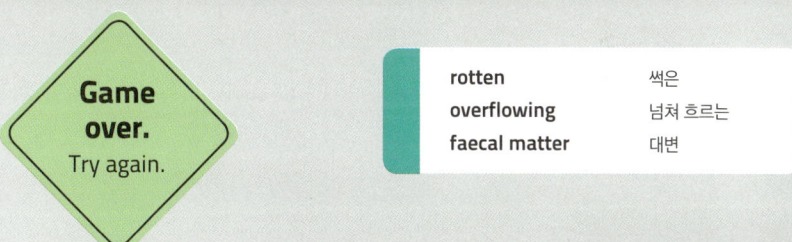

rotten	썩은
overflowing	넘쳐 흐르는
faecal matter	대변

D: All right, you'll get 30%.
A: Of what amount?
O: David, 10% would be more than plenty for that jerk!
A: I'm not taking any less than 30% and that does it! But how much is it?
D: Roughly speaking – 500,000 pounds!
A: 500,000 pounds! I knew you and your crooked cop were onto something big!

jerk	얼간이	**be onto**	~의 잘못을 적발하다
roughly speaking	어림잡아 말하자면	**dirty secret**	불명예스러운 비밀
crooked cop	부패한 경찰		

Grammar explanations

혼합가정법 Mixed Conditionals

→ 가정법 과거는 현재나 미래의 가상적인 상황에 대해 진술한다:

If I **had** a gun, I **would punish** Robert Murray straight away.
제게 총이 있다면 저는 당장 Robert Murray를 응징하겠어요.

→ 가정법 과거완료는 과거의 가정적인 상황에 대해 진술한다:

If Olive **had rejected** the call in the very first scene, we **would have never seen** so many adventures.   Olive가 첫 번째 장면에서 전화 통화를 거부했다면 우리는 그처럼 많은 모험담을 접하지 못했을 것입니다.

→ 과거의 사건으로 인한 현재의 결과에 대해 진술할 때에는, 아래와 같은 혼합가정법의 형태를 사용한다:

If + 주어 + 과거완료, 주어 + *would* + 부정사

If Olive **had rejected** (과거의 상황) the call in the very first scene, she **would not be** in trouble **now** (현재의 결과).
Olive가 첫 번째 장면에서 전화 통화를 거부했다면 그녀는 지금 곤경에 빠져 있지 않을 것입니다.

If Olive **hadn't come** (과거의 상황) across David, she **wouldn't have** such a good sidekick **now** (현재의 결과).
Olive가 David와 마주치지 않았다면 그녀에게는 지금 그처럼 뛰어난 조수가 없을 것입니다.

→ 영구적인 상태로 인한 과거의 결과에 대해 진술할 때에는, 아래와 같은 혼합 가정법의 형태를 사용한다:

If + 주어 + 과거, 주어 + *would* + *have* + 과거분사

If Olive **weren't** (영구적인 상태) so attractive, David **would not have forgotten** (과거의 결과) that he was a police officer.
Olive가 그처럼 매력적이지 않다면, David는 자신이 경찰관이었다는 사실을 잊지 않았을 것입니다.

If Robert **weren't** (영구적인 상태) such a ruthless person, he **wouldn't have brought** (과거의 결과) Beatrice to such a state.
Robert가 그처럼 무자비한 사람이 아니라면, 그는 Beatrice를 그와 같은 상태로 만들지 않았을 것입니다.

Communication situations

Read the following dialogues between activists involved in social campaigns.

Have you looked at new project applications for social campaigns? It's such a pity we can't finance all of them.

Dialogue 1

B: True, but here's one that really caught my attention.

A: Well, why don't we have a look at that now?

B: The one which concerns genetically modified food looks promising.

A: But do you want to be in favour or against it?

B: Well, the pro group promised us a sizeable donation if we organise a campaign in their favour.

A: Excuse me? Since when do we pick campaigns based on bribes?

---

bribe 뇌물 | **catch attention** 관심을 끌다 | **donation** 기부 | **genetically modified food (GMO)** 유전자 조작 식품

Dialogue 2

B: I'm not sure I understand you. All social campaigns are positive. That's a given.

A: Of course, but not all the issues we focus on have to be painful.

B: What brought that on? You realise that making people uncomfortable is practically in our job description?

A: I just can't take all that violence and tragedy anymore.

B: All right, I know it can be tough, but let's not get carried away. What we do is important.

---

social campaign 사회적 캠페인 | **That's a given.** 당연한 것이다. | **What brought that on?** 왜 그렇게 된 거죠? | **job description** 직무 해설서; 업무 | **make uncomfortable** 불편하게 만들다

Vocabulary plus

a good place to start 좋은 출발점

adequate preparation 적절한 준비

alienation 멀리함

among ~ 사이에

angle 각도

antibiotic resistance 항생제 내성

armed conflict 무력 분쟁

balanced 안정된

be that as it may 그렇기는 하지만

bio-weapon 세균성 무기

body image 신체상

boob job 유방 확대 수술

botched 망친

break through 돌파하다, 극복하다

burning 시급한

cancer patients and survivors 암 환자들과 생존자들

cause 원인

complacency 현 상태에 만족함, 안주함

complacent 안주하는

currently 현재의

danger 위험

decline 쇠퇴

dilemma 딜레마

discrimination 차별

elderly 어르신

ever-present 항상 존재하는

extreme case 극단적인 경우

food supply 식량공급

form the basis of ~의 토대를 이루다

get better 나아지다

get priority 우선권을 갖다

government 정부

high-calibre issue 높은 수준의 문제

higher risk 더 높은 위험

hypocrite 위선자

immune system 면역체계

improve 향상시키다

in practical terms 현실적으로 말하자면

in that aspect 그런 면에서는

in the small hours of the morning 새벽에

inequity 불공평

interact 소통하다

isolate 격리하다

isolation 격리

It can't go on like that. 이렇게 내버려 둘 수는 없다.

launch 착수하다

light 가벼운, 간단한

Make hay while the sun shines. 기회가 왔을 때 최선을 다 하라.

marginalize 사회적으로 무시하다

mental condition 정신적인 상태

- **mental disorder** 정신 장애
- **mental health** 정신 건강
- **negative** 결점
- **obtain** 입수하다, 구하다
- **off the top of one's head** 당장 생각나는 것으로는
- **old age** 노년; 노령
- **opponent** 상대, 반대자
- **opportunist** 기회주의자
- **outstanding** 뛰어난
- **oversimplification** 지나친 단순화
- **overworked** 혹사당하는
- **party** 정당
- **plastic surgery** 성형수술
- **point** 가리키다
- **positive effect** 긍정적인 효과
- **preferably** 가급적이면
- **pressing** 긴급한
- **rage** 급속히 번지다
- **rapidly growing number** 빠르게 증가하는 수치
- **reminder** (상기시키기 위한) 주의, 신호
- **resistant to** ~에 대해 저항하는
- **resulting** 결과로 초래된
- **security services** 보안 기관
- **see coming** 오는 것을 보다
- **society** 사회
- **solid** 확실한
- **suicide** 자살
- **taboo** 금기
- **take a different approach** 다른 접근법을 쓰다
- **The jury is still out.** 아직 평가가 내려지지 않았다.
- **to last me a lifetime** 인생에서 마지막으로
- **underscore** 밑줄 표시하다
- **urgent** 긴급한
- **value** 소중하게 생각하다
- **Western societies** 서구 사회
- **youth** 어린 시절
- **You've got my blessing.** 축복받으세요.

Cultural tips

Did you know that …?

A genetically modified organism (GMO) is an organism whose genetic material has been altered using genetic engineering techniques.

Scene 6 (54) — Film dialogue and vocabulary

Read the dialogue between Murray (M) and Gennady (G). Check the list of words and phrases below.

I expected you'd deal with the matter in a somewhat smarter way!

M: The bodies were supposed to have been got rid of! And what do you do? Plant cocaine on them! Now my employees are under suspicion of having been drug traffickers! How is that helping me keep a low profile?

G: You did not give us enough time! The police were minutes away and the boys happened to have some coke in the car! Now … tell me – how deep in shit are we?

M: I've already been called on by a police officer inquiring …

G: I asked: "How deep in shit are we?".

M: The disk contains some records from the early stages of our cooperation. They pertain to the front groups we set up to shield your work here. I assure you, though, it contains no data about the money-laundering operations we … carried out!

level C1

Vocabulary

somewhat	어느 정도	records	기록
plant	몰래 넣어 두다	stage	단계
cocaine	코카인	pertain (to)	관련하다
be under suspicion	혐의를 받다	front group	위장 회사
drug trafficker	마약 밀매자	shield	가리다, 보호하다
keep a low profile	이목을 피하다	assure	장담하다
coke	코카인	money-laundering	돈세탁
be deep in shit	어려운 지경이 되다	operation	작전, 활동
inquire	문의하다	carry out	수행하다
contain	포함하다		

I don't understand! Am I in danger or am I not?

What should Murray do?

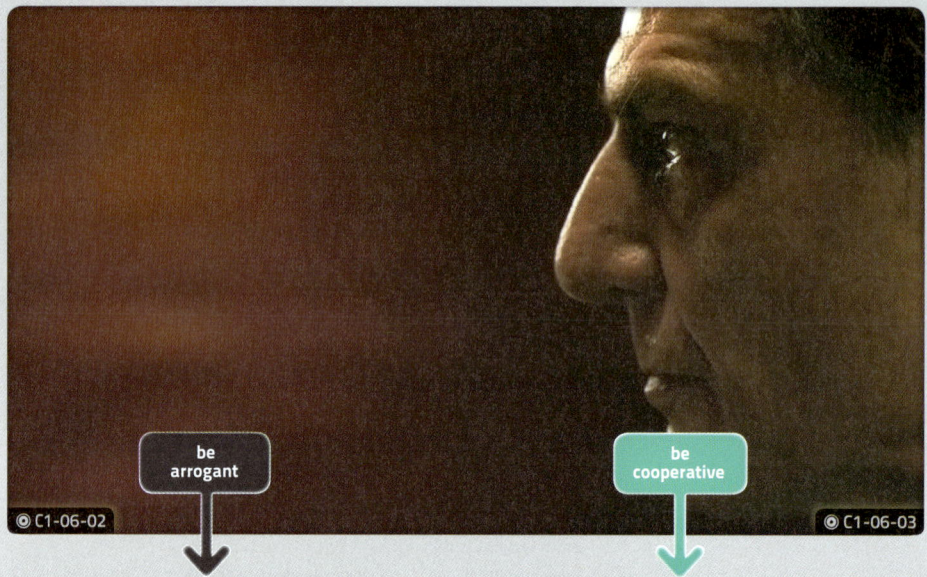

be arrogant

be cooperative

M: It depends on how much effort you put into keeping me safe! Do you understand, my Russian friend?

Game over.
Try again.

| put effort in | 노력을 기울이다 |

M: We both are, but this can be solved if we work together. Gennady, we've been doing business for over 20 years! We're friends, for Christ's sake! Let's put our heads together, find a way to clean up this mess and go back to making money!

G: You might be right! Well, the obvious way out of this is killing them all. Anyone who's involved or may be involved, the girl, her boyfriend, their associates, all of them.

M: Yes, all of them! … And Allen Adams!

G: Who? (…)

A: Olive, does the name Allen Adams ring a bell?

| ring a bell | 들어본 적이 있다 |

Grammar explanations

수동형 Passive forms

부정사가 포함된 수동태 = 주어 + be + 과거분사 + to be + 과거분사:

The judge **is to prepare** the ruling. → The ruling is **to be prepared** by the judge.
판사가 판결을 준비할 것입니다. → 판결은 판사에 의해 준비될 것입니다.

We **expect** that the police **will question** the suspects. → The suspects are expected **to be questioned**.
우리는 경찰이 용의자들을 심문할 것이라고 예상합니다. → 용의자들은 심문을 받을 것으로 예상됩니다.

The authorities **are supposed to examine** major evidence. → Major evidence is supposed **to be examined** (by the authorities).
당국이 주요 증거를 검토할 것입니다. → 주요 증거가 (당국에 의해) 검토될 것입니다.

수동형 부정사는 주로 아래의 경우에 사용된다:
➜ 다음 동사들의 뒤에서: seem, want, expect, need, hope, be supposed to
➜ 다음 표현들의 뒤에서: It's the first / second / last / etc. (+ noun)

His friends and employees are **expected to be questioned** soon.
그의 친구들과 직원들이 곧 심문을 받을 것으로 예상됩니다.

All available evidence will **need to be examined** by the authorities.
구할 수 있는 모든 증거는 당국에 의해 검토되어야 할 것입니다.

Robert Murray was **the first suspect to be visited** by the police.
Robert Murray는 경찰의 방문을 받은 첫 번째 용의자였습니다.

Olive is **the last person to be fooled** by people such as Murray.
Olive는 결코 Murray와 같은 사람들에게 속을 사람이 아닙니다.

동명사를 취하는 동사의 뒤에는 수동형 동명사가 뒤따른다: 주어 + 동사 + being + 과거분사:

David likes when people tell him the truth. → David **likes being told** the truth.
David는 사람들이 자신에게 진실을 말하는 것을 좋아합니다. → David는 진실을 듣는 것을 좋아합니다.

Olive doesn't mind it when employers give her difficult tasks. → Olive doesn't **mind being given** difficult tasks.
Olive는 고용주들이 어려운 임무를 주어도 꺼리지 않습니다. → Olive는 어려운 임무를 받는 것을 꺼리지 않습니다.

Vlad doesn't enjoy it when they send him to foreign countries. → Vlad doesn't **enjoy being sent** to foreign countries.
Vlad는 그들이 자신을 해외로 보내는 것을 좋아하지 않습니다. → Vlad는 해외로 보내지는 것을 좋아하지 않습니다.

완료형 수동태(to have been + 과거분사)는 과거에 누군가가 행위를 완료하지 못했거나 의무를 이행하지 못했음을 알릴 때 사용된다.

The bodies **were to be taken** away. → We know that somebody was supposed to remove them (that's all we know).
시체들은 치워져야 했습니다. → 우리는 누군가가 그것을 치워야 한다는 점을 알고 있습니다. (그것이 우리가 아는 전부입니다.)

The bodies **were to have been taken** away. ➔ We know that somebody was supposed to remove them but did not.
시체들은 치워져야 했습니다. → 우리는 누군가가 그것을 치워야 한다는 점을 알고 있지만 그렇게 되지는 않았습니다.

The warehouse **was supposed to be searched** for signs of a fight. ➔ We know it was somebody's duty to search it (that's all we know).
싸움의 흔적을 찾기 위해 창고가 수색되어야 했습니다. → 우리는 그곳을 조사하는 것이 누군가의 임무라는 점을 알고 있습니다. (그것이 우리가 아는 전부입니다.)

The warehouse **was supposed to have been searched** for signs of a fight. ➔ We know it was somebody's duty and we know this duty was neglected.
싸움의 흔적을 찾기 위해 창고가 수색되어야 했습니다. → 우리는 그것이 누군가의 임무라는 것을 알고 있고 그러한 임무가 수행되지 않았다는 점도 알고 있습니다.

Communication situations

Read the following dialogues between a couple planning their home budget. The husband has just lost his job.

We have to face it. I've lost my job. We have to reduce our spending to meet our monthly budget.

Dialogue 1

Wife: Honey, don't be so pessimistic. I'm sure you'll find another one soon.

Husband: Honey, be realistic. The labour market is full of key account managers. I'm not saying it's impossible but for sure it won't be easy to get a job with equally good working conditions.

Wife: Are you trying to say that our standard of living might be lower?

Husband: That's exactly what I'm saying.

Wife: Good! I'm tired of keeping up with the Joneses.

Husband: Are you? You should have told me that! It would have been much easier for us.

---

key account manager 핵심 고객 관리자 | **standard of living** 생활 수준

Communication situations

Dialogue 2

Wife: All right, let's do a bit of home accounting.

Husband: So what do we have?

Wife: We've got a mortgage and generally we are in the red.

Husband: Yes, I remember. Let's start with the money we've got in hand, shall we?

Wife: We've got some cash in the bank.

Husband: Honey, if it's in the bank, it's not cash.

Wife: Somebody is being picky here!

be in the red 적자이다 I **picky** 까다로운

Dialogue 3

Husband: Let's make a balance sheet.

Wife: A balance sheet? Aren't you exaggerating a bit?

Husband: So what do you suggest?

Wife: Well, my salary will cover the basic expenditures but we cannot afford any holidays or renovations.

Husband: Oh come on. We've been saving up for the last couple of months. I'm sure we can spend the money on one of those things.

Wife: If I were to choose, I'd go for holidays although I'm still not convinced about this idea.

Husband: We've been working hard. We deserve a holiday - and what's more, we need it.

Wife: You're right. I could do without it but we have promised the kids to go somewhere.

Husband: And that's the strongest argument in favour of going, yes.

balance sheet 대차대조표 I **expenditure** 지출 I **renovation** 개조, 보수

Dialogue 4

Wife: Are you worried about the money or about the job?

Husband: Well, one goes with the other, doesn't it?

Wife: You haven't answered my question.

Husband: The money.

Wife: Let me remind you that I also contribute to our home budget.

Husband: Of course you do. But we won't make ends meet on just your salary.

home budget 가계 예산 | **make ends meet** 겨우 먹고 살 만큼 벌다

Vocabulary plus

accounting 회계

acquit 무죄를 선고하다

assigned 할당된, 배정된

avoid 피하다

blow (돈을) 펑펑 쓰다

board meeting 이사회

circles 집단

coach 코치

cut down on ~을 줄이다

differ 다르다

drop 그만두다

embezzlement 횡령, 착복

good society 상류층

gross slander 중상, 모략

household 가정

income 수입

ins and outs 수입과 지출

insider trading 내부자거래

interest 이자

leisure activities 레저 활동

long-term investment 장기 투자

meet the budget 예산에 맞추다

ostracized 외면된

preliminary results 예비적 결과

put off 연기하다

reach the peak 절정에 이르다

sales reps training 영업사원교육

savings account 저축예금계좌

securities 증권

separately 따로따로

socks 양말

sources of financing 자금의 원천

spending 소비

stand trial 재판을 받다

stock exchange 증권거래소

stocks 주식

sue 소송을 제기하다

take the bull by the horns 정면으로 맞서다

that being so 그래서

tighten the belt 긴축재정을 하다

time off 휴식

undervalue 과소평가하다

worry 걱정

Cultural tips

Did you know that ...?

"Keeping up with the Joneses" is an idiom in many parts of the English-speaking world referring to the comparison to one's neighbour as a benchmark for social class and material goods. The phrase originated in a comic strip of the same name authored by Arthur R. "Pop" Momand.

Scene 7 (55)   Film dialogue and vocabulary

Read the dialogue between David and Alfie. Check the list of words and phrases below.

| break into | 무단 침입하다 |
| search warrant | 수색 영장 |

60   Olive Green

level C1

Read Alfie's monologue. Check the list of words and phrases below.

Gosh, you don't have much sympathy for drinkers, do you? Do I sense a childhood trauma?

sympathy	동정심	**childhood**	어린 시절
drinker	술꾼	**trauma**	트라우마, 정신적 외상
sense	느끼다		

Read the dialogue between Alfie (A), David (D) and Adams (AA). Check the list of words and phrases below.

I'm not telling you anything. The only reason I'm still alive is I've kept my mouth shut!

A: Opening it only when there was booze to be drunk!
D: Why did Robert Murray pay you 10,000 pounds?

All right! You leave me no choice!

Stop it! I'll tell you everything. Leave at least one full, please!

AA: He knew I was hard up at that time, paying child maintenance and … drinking. He said he was planning to stage an accident and claim the insurance money. He assured me it was his own car. I saw him driving it, okay? So I thought, why not? The guy knows what he's doing. So I tinkered with the brakes a bit. I didn't know he was planning to kill them!

D: Kill who?

AA: The Campbells – the rich folk from Old Berry!

A: The guy hired you to kill his own in-laws?

AA: I didn't kill them! I just … I so regret having listened to him! … He later warned me not to say a word about it! So I didn't! Not for 27 years. … Can I get my drink now?

Vocabulary				
	open	입을 열다	tinker with	~을 만지작거리다
	child maintenance	자녀 양육비	brake	브레이크
	stage	(일을) 벌이다	folk	사람들
	accident	사고	in-laws	시부모/처부모
	claim	청구하다	regret	후회하다
	insurance	보험금	warn	경고하다

Grammar explanations

동명사나 부정사를 취하는 동사 / 둘 다 취하는 동사 / 다양한 형태
Verbs followed by -ing or infinitive or both or with various patterns

→ 동사 + to부정사 = 동사 + 동명사

begin, start, continue 등과 같은 몇몇 동사들은 의미의 변화 없이 to부정사와 동명사를 모두 취할 수 있다.

The currency rate was favourable so Gennady **started** to invest / investing his dirty money.   환율이 유리해서 Gennady는 그의 부정한 돈을 투자하기 시작했습니다.

I don't mind criticism. I am going **to continue** to write / writing my second novel anyway.   비판은 신경 쓰지 않아요. 어쨌든 저는 계속해서 제 두 번째 소설을 쓸 거예요.

→ 동사 + to부정사 ≠ 동사 + 동명사

어떤 동사들은 to부정사나 동명사를 취할 수 있지만, 각각의 경우 의미가 다르다:

remember to do – 어떠한 행동을 할 것을 잊지 않는다
It was funny when Vlad didn't **remember** to pay for his shirt.
Vlad가 셔츠 값을 내야 한다는 것을 잊다니 재미있었어요.

remember doing – 과거의 행동을 기억한다
Yes, he's a funny character. I can **remember** him doing more crazy things.
네, 그는 재미있는 캐릭터예요. 저는 그가 훨씬 말도 안 되는 행동을 했던 것이 기억나요.

regret to do – 발생할 일에 대해 유감이다
I **regret** to say that your mother will lose her B&B if you don't cooperate.
당신이 협조하지 않으면 당신의 어머니가 B&B를 잃게 될 것이라는 말씀을 드리게 되어 유감입니다.

regret doing something – 과거의 일에 대해 유감이다
I guess Gennady **regrets** not seeing his son for so long.
저는 Gennady가 그처럼 오랫동안 자신의 아들을 만나지 못한 것을 후회하고 있다고 생각해요.

stop to do something – (대개 다른 행동을 하기 위해) 하던 행동을 멈추다
As Olive and David were digging the grave, David **stopped** to take a look around.
Olive와 David가 무덤을 파고 있을 때, David는 일을 잠시 멈추고 주변을 둘러보았습니다.

stop doing something – 하던 일을 그만 두다
Alfie says he **stopped** smoking but he doesn't mind having one more cigarette, all the same.   Alfie는 담배를 끊었다고 하지만, 그럼에도 불구하고, 언제나 담배를 한 개 더 가지고 있는 것은 신경 쓰지 않아요.

→ 어떤 동사들은 to부정사나 동명사를 취할 수 있다. 그 결과 의미가 변화한다:

forget to do – 어떤 것에 신경 써야 하는 것을 기억하지 못하다
Do you remember when Olive **forgot** to hide her laptop and David found it?
Olive가 노트북을 숨기는 것을 잊어서 David가 그것을 발견했다는 점이 기억나요?

forget doing – 과거의 순간을 기억하지 못하다
Did she? Oh, yes, she did! I completely **forgot** watching that scene!
그녀가 그랬어요? 오, 네, 그랬죠! 그 장면을 보았다는 것을 완전히 잊고 있었어요!

try to do – ~하려고 노력하다

Olive should **try to prepare** her heists in a more creative way. That thing with Curtis was below her skills.
Olive는 보다 창의적인 방식으로 도둑질을 준비하도록 노력해야 해요. Curtis의 도둑질은 그녀보다 수준이 낮았어요.

try doing – ~을 시도하다

She's good with computers, so perhaps she should **try hacking** the security system first.   그녀는 컴퓨터에 능하기 때문에 아마 우선적으로 보안 시스템을 해킹하려고 할 거예요.

mean to do – ~할 의도이다

David is such a naive young man. What do you think he **means to do** next?
David는 정말 순진한 사람이에요. 그가 이 다음에 무엇을 할 것 같나요?

mean doing – ~을 의미하다

He will do everything to protect Olive, even if it **means shooting** somebody.
그는 Olive를 보호하기 위해서라면 어떤 일이라도 할 거예요, 그것이 누군가를 쏘는 일을 의미하는 경우라도요.

→ 몇몇 동사들은(e.g.: *see, hear, avoid, deny, miss*) 주로 목적어와 동명사를 함께 취한다.

The security guard didn't **see** David **sneaking** up to him.
경비원은 David가 자신에게 몰래 다가오는 것을 알지 못했어요.

Olive was conversing with Alfie, when suddenly she **heard** Cloutier **saying** her name.
Olive는 Alfie와 대화를 나누고 있었는데, 그때 갑자기 Cloutier가 자신의 이름을 말하는 것을 들었어요.

→ 몇몇 동사들은(e.g.: *let, make, help*) 항상 목적어와 부정사를 함께 취한다.

Marco, the scary brute with a gun, didn't **let** Olive and David **escape**.
Marco는, 총을 든 무시무시한 야수 같았는데, Olive와 David가 탈출하게 놔두지 않았습니다.

However, the duo **made** him **change** his mind and left him bleeding on the floor.
하지만 그 두 사람은 그가 마음을 바꾸도록 만들었고 그가 바닥에서 피를 흘리도록 놔두었습니다.

이러한 패턴은 수동태에서 변화한다.

주어 + be동사 (적절한 시제) + made + to + 부정사

Marco was **made to change** his mind by Olive and David.
Marco는 Olive와 David에 의해 마음이 바뀌었습니다.

Beatrice wasn't **allowed to marry** Martin by her ruthless parents.
Beatrice는 인정 없는 그녀의 부모에게 Martin과의 결혼을 허락받지 못했습니다.

Communication situations

Read the following dialogues between two friends discussing their current projects.

Hi, sorry I'm late. I hope you haven't been waiting too long. What are you reading?

Dialogue 1

Man: Hi, how are you? I'm working on my project.

Woman: Ah, the mysterious project. When are you going to lift the curtain on it?

Man: How about now? I'm going to stand as a candidate in the municipal elections.

Woman: Really? I don't know what to say.

Man: Well, you can offer to stand by my side, for starters.

Woman: I will, of course I will. But why? I mean what made you consider this path?

Man: I want to finally call a spade a spade.

Woman: What do you mean?

Man: I'm going to provide free nursery and elderly care for the people in the village.

Woman: And end world hunger, while you're at it.

Man: I beg your pardon?

Woman: Sorry, I don't mean to hurt you. But it might be impossible to keep such election promises.

lift the curtain (on) 공개하다 I **stand as a candidate** 후보로 출마하다 I **municipal elections** 시의원 선거 I **stand by somebody's side** ~의 편에 서다 I **call a spade a spade** 자기 생각을 그대로 말하다 I **care** 돌봄, 보살핌 I **world hunger** 전 세계적인 기아 I **while you're at it** 자리에 있을 때 I **keep election promises** 선거 공약을 지키다

Dialogue 2

Man: Hi, it's nice to see you. I've been studying the regulations of one of the social websites.

Woman: Why? It's just a set of rules written by some lawyers. Nobody reads that.

Man: That's the point. People are not familiar with the rules they agree to.

Woman: Why do you always want to save other people from themselves? It's their problem, isn't it?

Man: It becomes mine when my child joins a social network.

Woman: Isn't he too young to go on the net? I mean, to create an account and so on.

Man: And how can such a system really verify somebody's age?

Woman: There should be some safety measures in place. At least I imagine there are.

be familiar with ~을 잘 알게 되다 I **social network** 소셜 네트워크 I **verify** 확인하다 I **safety measures** 안전 조치 I **be in place** 준비되어 있다

Dialogue 3

Man: I'm just thinking of starting some association or foundation, that's all.

Woman: So you haven't decided on the legal status of it yet?

Man: No, not yet.

Woman: All right, you still have time, I guess. What is it going to be about?

Man: This town needs some regular events. And I need to find people interested in helping me to organise them.

Woman: Then maybe you should consider setting up an event agency, not a foundation. There should be some money in it, at least.

foundation 재단 I **set up** 설립하다

Vocabulary plus

activate 활동적이게 하다

at any point 어떠한 관점에서도

bathing suit 수영복

be of assistance 도움이 되다

bring some fresh air to 주의를 환기시키다

come as a surprise 예상하지 못한 일이다

constantly 끊임없이

content 내용

dark horse 다크호스, 복병

elsewhere 어딘가에서

excerpt 발췌

general public 일반 대중

go over 검토하다

inspiration 영감

interrupt the train of thought 생각의 흐름을 방해하다

join 가입하다

keep an eye on ~을 계속 지켜보다

leave a trace 흔적을 남기다

legal entity 법적 실체

mandate 권한

neglected 방치된

non-attached 소속되지 않은

occasionally 때때로

parental control 자녀 보호 설정

pic 사진

print out 출력하다

privacy 사생활

psycho 정신병자

put in danger 위험에 빠뜨리다

raise the hackles 화나게 하다

responsibly 책임감 있게

rights and obligations 권리와 의무

rock the boat 평지풍파를 일으키다

scary prospect 두려운 전망

self-conceited 자부심이 강한

social life 사회 생활

take a step back from ~에서 한 걸음 물러서다

tax system 조세 제도

There's no guarantee ... ~한다는 보장은 없다

transfer the copyright to 저작권을 넘기다

unemployment 실업

update 갱신하다

upload 업로드하다

user 사용자

viewable 볼 수 있는, 보이는

what's got into you today? 왜 그러니?

wing 계파, 진영

Cultural tips

Did you know that ...?

In English, "in-laws" means a parent of your husband or wife or a member of his or her family. You can use more specific terms to point to a particular relative, for example: mother-in-law, father-in-law, brother-in-law, sister-in-law etc.

Scene 8 (56)   Film dialogue and vocabulary

Read the dialogue between Gennady (G), Yuri (Y) and Vlad (V).
Check the list of words and phrases below.

Aha! ... Okay, follow the copper and keep me posted! We'll meet you at their place!

Y: Boss, do you want us to finish Adams off before we go for the girl and her team?

G: I think not! Not yet, at least!

Y: But Murray swore that the guy is a ticking time bomb!

G: You see, lads, I'm increasingly reluctant to believe anything that man says. He fancies himself cunning as a fox, but that is not quite true! My instincts tell me that he is losing his grip on things. Oh well, it seems our long-standing cooperation will need to be terminated.

V: A complicated sentence! Are we killing our British lawyer or not?

G: We just might, Vlad. Okay, Yuri, drive!

Vocabulary

copper	경찰관	fancy oneself as	~라고 자부하다
keep posted	계속 알려 주다	cunning as a fox	여우처럼 약은
finish off	~을 죽이다	one's instincts tell ...	본능에 따르면 ~이다
swear	욕을 하다	lose one's grip (on)	능력을 잃다
ticking time bomb	시한폭탄	long-standing	장기간의
lad	친구들	terminate	종료하다
be reluctant	꺼려하다	sentence	문장
increasingly	점점 더	drive	운전하다

level C1

Read the dialogue between Olive (O) and Alfie (A). Check the list of phrases below.

- Yeah?
- Stop wasting your time with that disk!

A: We found something out! Listen! Murray hired Allen Adams to kill his in-laws.
O: Okay ... I think I have an idea. We'll talk when you're back.

waste one's time
~의 시간을 허비하다

Read the dialogue between Beatrice (B) and Olive (O). Check the list of words and phrases below.

- Hello?
- This is Olive Green. Do you remember me?

B: How could I forget you? The quick-witted girl that made a fool out of my son and husband. What is it that you want from me?

| quick-witted | 머리가 잘 돌아가는 | make a fool of | ~을 바보로 만들다 |

level C1 Scene 8 (56) 71

What should Olive do?

ask for help

make a proposal

O: I need your help to deal with your husband.

B: I'm sorry dear, I learnt a long time ago never to cross Robert. You're on your own, Olive. Good luck, though!

O: I have a great proposal that can change your life!

B: Can it? Well then, I'm all ears because I'm quite ready for a new start.

| be all ears | 열심히 귀를 기울이다 |

Game over.
Try again.

| cross | 속이다, 배신하다 |

Grammar explanations

직유법 Similes

직유법은 유사함을 표현하는 비유적인 표현이다. 주로 아래의 두 가지 유형 중 하나를 취한다:

동사 + **like** + 명사
(**as**) + 형용사 + **as** + 명사

Is it true that when he is in Moscow, Vlad **drinks like a fish**? → Does he drink a lot in Moscow?   Vlad가 모스크바에 있을 때 마치 물고기처럼 술을 마신다는 것이 사실인가요? → 그가 모스크바에서 술을 많이 마시나요?

You never know what Olive may come up with. The girl is **like a volcano**. → She is unpredictable and explosive by temperament.   Olive가 어떤 생각을 떠올릴지는 결코 알 수 없어요. 그 여자는 마치 화산 같거든요. → 그녀는 예측하기 힘들며 기분에 따라 흥분을 잘 해요.

It seems a lost cause, but David still follows Olive. The guy **is as stubborn as a mule**. → He is very stubborn and obstinate.   승산이 없어 보이지만 아직도 David는 Olive를 따르고 있어요. 그 남자는 마치 당나귀처럼 고집이 세죠. → 그는 고집이 세고 완고해요.

복합 형용사 Compound adjectives

복합 형용사는 두 부분으로 구성되는데, 하이픈으로 연결되어 있다.

> 명사 +

a **stress-free** occupation → 명사 + 형용사
a **hair-raising** experience → 명사 + 현재분사
a **man-made** structure → 명사 + 과거분사

> 형용사 +

a **last-minute** holiday → 형용사 + 명사
a **long-standing** cooperation → 형용사 + 과거분사
a **hand-picked** crew → 형용사 + 과거분사

> 부사 +

a **well-deserved** prize → 부사 + 과거분사

Communication situations

Read the following dialogues between an investor and a beginning entrepreneur.

Before you start your presentation, let me remind you that you are one of five start-ups that we are going to assess in terms of their credibility and financial prospects. Now, the floor is yours.

Dialogue 1

Entrepreneur: Thank you. Ladies and gents, I'm not going to start my presentation now.

Investor: You are not?

Entrepreneur: No. I'd like you to answer a question for me.

Investor: Interesting approach. What's the question?

Entrepreneur: What is the thing that you don't need?

Investor: Are you asking me personally or the other members of the jury?

Entrepreneur: That's the thing. Each of you would give a different answer.

Investor: Well, that idea is not exactly revolutionary. What's your point?

Entrepreneur: Forgetting about trends and thinking out of the box.

Investor: I don't want to disappoint you but we hear a similar phrase in every other presentation. How is your idea different from the others?

Entrepreneur: Personalised shopping for the sustainable lifestyle enthusiasts.

Investor: All right. You are an interesting candidate, but you need to provide us with more details. Come again on Wednesday.

approach 접근 | revolutionary 혁신적인 | sustainable lifestyle 안정적인 라이프스타일 | enthusiast 열성적인 사람

Dialogue 2

Entrepreneur: First, let me thank you all for inviting me to the second round of the programme.

Investor: Well, you intrigued us. Let's see how you do in this part.

Entrepreneur: I'm pleased to hear it. So let's start the ball rolling.

Investor: Yes, let's. So. Financing. Money. And the big question – how to get it?

Entrepreneur: The first stage of my start-up's development was supported by European Union grants and ministry subventions.

Investor: Well done. These are excellent sources of financial backing. Now, what do you expect from us?

Entrepreneur: I'm about to start mass production and I need capital for the first year of operating.

Investor: That's quite unusual. What return on equity do you expect to have after that year?

Entrepreneur: The realistic scenario is about 15% after the first year.

Investor: Yes, that's a reasonable assumption. Now, let's talk about your growth prediction for the next three to five years.

intrigue 호기심을 불러 일으키다 | **start-up** 창업 단계의 기업 | **ministry subventions** 정부 보조금 | **backing** 지원 | **mass production** 대량 생산 | **capital** 자본금 | **operating** 가동 | **return on equity** 자기자본수익률 | **prediction** 예측

Dialogue 3

Entrepreneur: What's the point? You are chiefly interested in the amount of money I want, not in my project.

Investor: Well, according to the regulations of the Young Entrepreneurs Programme we should know the businesses we support. But OK. Lay your cards on the table, please.

Entrepreneur: Fair enough. What would you say if I didn't ask you for money, but for patronage?

Investor: Young man, you are turning this meeting upside down. You want us to play by your rules.

patronage 후원 | **turn upside down** ~을 엉망으로 만들다

Vocabulary plus

accordingly 부응해서, 그에 맞춰

allocate 배분하다

allure 매력

arrangement 준비

assess 가늠하다, 평가하다

assistant 조수; 보조원

bank loan 은행 융자금

calculation 계산

Call it what you will. 당신 좋을 대로 부르세요.

collect 수집하다

competitive advantage 경쟁우위

competitive strategy 경쟁전략

concept 개념

conclusion 결과

customisable 주문 제작 가능한

enterprise 기업

establish 설립하다

fashion 패션

feel obliged 의무감이 들다

financial prospects 재정전망

financial security 재정보증

fledgling 초보자

How refreshingly straightforward! 신선할 정도로 간단하다!

in the pipeline 한창 진행 중인

initial 초기의

Is that so? 그렇습니까?

launching the product on the market 시장에 상품을 출시하다

low-interest 낮은 금리

make the best use of 최대한 활용하다

marketing campaign 마케팅 전략

match 연결시키다

modify 수정하다, 변경하다

negotiate 협상하다

participate 참여하다

pour money into ~에 자금을 쏟아 붓다

raise one's interest in ~의 관심을 끌다

self-confidence 자신

stay in opposition 반대 입장을 취하다

target group 표적집단

The end justifies the means. 끝이 좋으면 다 좋다.

vague 모호한

wishful thinking 희망사항

Cultural tips

Did you know that ...?

In English, there are several useful idioms with the word "end":

The end justifies the means. (used to describe a situation in which the final aim is so important that any way of achieving it is acceptable)

To make ends meet. (used to say that someone earns and spends equal amounts of money)

All's well that ends well. (used to describe an event that has a good ending even if some things went wrong along the way)

Scene 9 (57)   Film dialogue and vocabulary

Read the dialogue between David (D), Alfie (A), Olive (O) and Gennady (G). Check the list of words and phrases below.

> If this isn't time we called the police, then I don't know what is! We've got strong evidence and Adams is ready to testify!

> Yeah, it's enough to dangle a bottle in front of his eyes!

O: No!

D: Then what would you have me do?

O: Count on me to unravel this mess.

D: What?

A: The pony-tail geezer there is Gennady Korolyov. Head of the UK branch of the biggest Russian mafia family. The guy next to him is his right-hand man, Yuri – one of the meanest, most sadistic thugs in the whole of London! As for the really big guy … I don't suppose he's a Bolshoi Ballet dancer touring the UK. … Okay, Alfie, think … It was lovely to meet you, David. Under different circumstances I am sure we'd have been the best of pals! Olive, dear Olive, you could have been the love of my life, but at this point I think I need to be selfish in a healthy way! I think it weird that we should all die when I don't have to. So, good luck!

O: David, no! Trust me – I've got this under control! Let me talk to them!

D: Okay, Olive. You're on! (…) Just in case I never get another chance!

level C1

Vocabulary				
evidence	증거	mean	사나운, 지독한
testify	증언하다	sadistic	가학적인
dangle	달랑거리다	ballet	발레
bottle	병	dancer	댄서
count on	~을 믿다	tour	순회
unravel	풀다, 해결하다	circumstances	상황
pony-tail	뒤로 묶은 머리	pal	친구
geezer	남자	selfish	이기적인
branch	지사, 지부	healthy	건전한
mafia	마피아	be on	~을 맡다
right-hand man	오른팔 (중요한 인물)		

Oh boy, where to start?

level C1 Scene 9 (57)

Grammar explanations

가주어 It   It as preparatory subject

To dangle a bottle in front of his eyes **is** enough.와 같이 표현할 수도 있지만 이러한 문장은 사용되는 경우가 거의 없고 부자연스럽다. **It is** enough to dangle a bottle in front of his eyes.와 같이 표현하는 것이 더 좋다.

Not to drink when you're on a job seems vital.
일을 하고 있을 때에는 술을 마시지 않는 것이 중요해 보입니다.

→ **It seems** vital not to drink when you're on a job.
일을 하고 있을 때에는 술을 마시지 않는 것이 중요해 보입니다.

To trust David now is important (for Olive). 지금 David를 믿는 것은 (Olive에게) 중요합니다.

→ **It is** important to trust David now. 지금 David를 믿는 것이 중요합니다.
→ **It is** important for Olive to trust David now. 지금 Olive가 David를 믿는 것이 중요합니다.

To take precautions was thoughtful. 예방 조치를 한 것은 사려 깊은 행동이었습니다.

→ **It was** thoughtful to take precautions. 예방 조치를 한 것은 사려 깊은 행동이었습니다.
→ **It was** thoughtful of you, Alfie, to take precautions.
Alfie, 당신이 예방 조치를 한 것은 사려 깊은 행동이었습니다.

It	+	is / was / has been / had been 또는 그 외의 동사 (will, seem, appear etc.)	+	형용사/ 부사	+	to부정사

It은 다른 부자연스러워 보이는 문장들에도 사용될 수 있다. 비교:

That somebody will get hurt in the final scenes appears probable.
마지막 장면에서 누군가 다칠 가능성이 높아 보입니다.

→ **It appears** probable <u>that</u> somebody will get hurt in the final scenes.
마지막 장면에서 누군가 다칠 가능성이 높아 보입니다.

That David will never win Olive's heart is obvious (to me).
David가 결코 Olive의 마음을 얻지 못할 것이라는 점은 (제게) 명백합니다.

→ **It is** obvious to me <u>that</u> David will never win Olive's heart.
David가 결코 Olive의 마음을 얻지 못할 것이라는 점은 제게 명백합니다.

Whether Alfie is a good or a bad guy remains uncertain.
Alfie가 좋은 사람인지, 혹은 나쁜 사람인지는 불확실한 채로 남아 있습니다.

→ **It remains** uncertain <u>whether/if</u> Alfie is a good or a bad guy.
Alfie가 좋은 사람인지, 혹은 나쁜 사람인지는 불확실한 채로 남아 있습니다.

What Murray wants is finally unimportant to Beatrice.
Murray가 원하는 것은 결국 Beatrice에게는 중요하지 않은 것입니다.

→ **It's finally** unimportant to Beatrice <u>what</u> Murray wants.
Murray가 원하는 것은 결국 Beatrice에게는 중요하지 않은 것입니다.

It	+	is / was / has been / had been 또는 그 외의 동사 (will, seem, appear etc.)	+	형용사/ 부사	+	절 (that, if/ whether, what, when, how etc.)

분열문에서의 *It*   *It* in cleft sentences

가주어 it은 문장의 특정 부분을 강조할 때 사용될 수 있다.

Olive tried to steal the Thistle Flowers from Robert Murray last week.
Olive는 지난 주에 Robert Murray의 '엉겅퀴 꽃'을 훔치려고 했습니다.

→ It was Olive who tried to steal the Thistle Flowers from Robert Murray last week.
지난 주에 Robert Murray의 '엉겅퀴 꽃'을 훔치려고 했던 사람은 바로 Olive였습니다.

→ It was the Thistle Flowers that Olive tried to steal from Robert Murray last week.
Olive가 지난 주에 Robert Murray로부터 훔치려고 한 것은 바로 '엉겅퀴 꽃'이었습니다.

→ It was Robert Murray that/whom Olive tried to steal the Thistle Flowers from.
Olive가 지난 주에 훔치려고 한 '엉겅퀴 꽃'은 바로 Robert Murray의 것이었습니다.

→ It was last week when Olive tried to steal the Thistle Flowers from Robert Murray.
Olive가 Robert Murray의 '엉겅퀴 꽃'을 훔치려고 했던 것은 바로 지난 주였습니다.

It	+	is / was / has been / had been	+	강조하고자 하는 정보	+	that, who/whom 또는 when으로 시작하는 절

가목적어 *It*   *It* as preparatory object

I **think** that David shows so much courage in the end strange.와 같이 표현할 수도 있지만 이와 같이 사용되는 경우는 거의 없고 부자연스럽다. I **think it** strange **that** David shows so much courage in the end.와 같이 표현하는 것이 더 좋다.

Alfie believes that they should all die when he doesn't have to is weird. → Alfie **believes it** weird **that** they should all die when he doesn't have to.   Alfie는 그가 그렇게 하지 않으면 그들이 모두 죽을 것이라는 점이 이상하다고 생각했습니다.

Apparently, he finds facing danger difficult. → Apparently, he **finds it** difficult to face danger.   분명, 그는 위험과 마주하는 것이 어려운 일이라는 점을 알고 있습니다.

Murray made what he wanted to happen to witnesses very clear. → Murray **made it** very clear **what** he wanted to happen to witnesses.   Murray는 그가 무엇을 목격하고자 했었는지를 매우 분명히 밝혔습니다.

주어	+	동사	+	it	+	형용사	+	to부정사 또는 that, what 등으로 시작하는 절

몇몇 동사들은 정해진 유형이 있다. 비교:

Olive **finds it** useful **that** Curtis is so vain – it makes her job easier.
Olive는 Curtis가 매우 자만심이 강하다는 점이 유용한 사실이라고 생각합니다. – 이는 그녀의 일을 보다 수월하게 만듭니다.

Olive **likes it that** Curtis is so vain – it makes her job easier.
Olive는 Curtis가 매우 자만심이 강하다는 점을 좋아합니다. – 이는 그녀의 일을 보다 수월하게 만듭니다.

주어	+	동사	+	it	+	that / when으로 시작하는 절

Do you **appreciate it** that the film is full of games?
영화에 많은 게임이 들어 있는 것을 높이 평가하시나요?

I **like it** when I can have fun and learn at the same time.
저는 재미를 느끼면서 동시에 배울 수 있으면 좋습니다.

We **hate it** when a language course is predictable and boring.
저희는 어학 수업이 뻔하고 지루한 것을 싫어합니다.

I **take it** that (= I assume that) learning English with Olive is fantastic.
저는 Olive와 함께 영어를 배우는 것이 굉장한 일이라고 생각합니다.

Communication situations

Read the following phone dialogues between a tax office clerk and an entrepreneur.

Good afternoon, Revenue and Customs. How may I help?

Dialogue 1

Entrepreneur: I set up a company and was told to register for VAT.

Clerk: That's right. If your taxable turnover is more than £81,000, you must register.

Entrepreneur: But I've just started and have no idea about my future turnover.

Clerk: OK. Then you'll need to register when you go over the threshold. Which is £81,000, at the moment. Have a nice day!

---

taxable 과세되는 | **turnover** 총매출 | **threshold** 한계점

Dialogue 2

Entrepreneur: Good afternoon, I'm calling about submitting a tax return. I need some details.

Clerk: All right. Are you a sole-trader or a limited company?

Entrepreneur: I'm a sole-trader.

Clerk: I'm afraid you can't do it on the phone. You have to either send the form by post or use your online account.

Entrepreneur: But I don't have an online account.

Clerk: Then I must ask you about your UTR number. But before I continue I must advise you that this call may be recorded for quality and training purposes.

Entrepreneur: Yes, I know. What is the UTR number?

Clerk: OK. Have you already registered for Self Assessment?

Entrepreneur: Yes, I have, and I've been waiting for the activation code for a couple of days now.

Clerk: Exactly. Your activation code should arrive within 7 working days. However, you should have received the Unique Taxpayer Reference number when registering.

Entrepreneur: OK. Thank you very much.

Clerk: Thank you for your call.

submit 제출하다 | tax return 소득신고서 | sole-trader 개인사업자 | limited company 유한회사 | on the phone 전화상으로 | by post 우편으로 | activation code 활성화 코드

Dialogue 3

Entrepreneur: Good afternoon, I would like to submit a tax return.

Clerk: I'm afraid you can't do it on the phone. You have to either send the form by post or use your online account.

Entrepreneur: But I can't log in.

Clerk: Then I must ask you about your UTR number. But before I continue I must advise you that this call may be recorded for quality and training purposes.

Entrepreneur: I don't agree to be recorded.

Clerk: All right. Unfortunately, in that case I cannot continue our conversation. Please contact your local HMRC office to help you.

Vocabulary plus

accountant 회계사

appoint an agent 대리인을 임명하다

authorize 권한을 부여하다

editable 편집 가능한

intuitive 직감에 의한

officer 관리, 직원

on behalf 대신하여

payer 납부자

Revenue and Customs (HMRC) 세관

self-employed 자영업을 하는

unrecognizable 알아 볼 수 없는

written authorization 서면 결재

Cultural tips

Did you know that ...?

The Godfather, originally published in 1969, is a famous crime novel written by Italian American author Mario Puzo. It tells the story of a fictional Mafia family based in New York City, headed by Don Vito Corleone. The novel covers the years 1945 to 1955, and also provides the back story of Vito Corleone from early childhood to adulthood. It inspired a 1972 film of the same name; and then two sequels were made in 1974 and 1990.

Scene 10 (58)   Film dialogue and vocabulary

Read the dialogue between Gennady (G), Olive (O) and Yuri (Y).
Check the list of words and phrases below.

G: Business-related, mostly, but on the personal level ... You've been a real pain in the backside. You've met my son, Sergey, haven't you? He's in Sudan. As he explained to me in his letter, he'll be helping charities dig water wells for the locals. Also, he insists that I atone for all the evil things I have done! I blame you for that! You stressed him out or he got mental after you punched him! As for the business part ... I have heard from a reliable source that you have come into possession of some information. Reputedly, it's the sort of information that may cast suspicion on the legality of my business.

O: Bullshit!

G: What?

O: The disk contains no data about your cooperation with Murray. He only told you that so that you save his skin by killing us. He knows we know something.

Y: Which is?

O: He killed his own in-laws which led to his wife's nervous breakdown ... which he used to formally take over the management of her property.

Y: Not bad!

G: That sneaky bastard! Still ... good to know we're safe! Okay, it's been nice talking to you.

level C1

Vocabulary

sound reason	타당한 이유	reputedly	소문에 의하면
business-related	일과 관련된	cast suspicion (on)	~에 혐의를 두다
level	수준, 단계	legality	합법성
pain in the backside	골칫거리	save one's skin	위기를 모면하다
letter	편지	lead (to)	~을 초래하다
water well	우물	nervous breakdown	신경 쇠약
insist (on / that)	주장하다	formally	정식으로
atone for	~에 대해 속죄하다	take over	인수하다
stress out	~에 스트레스를 주다	management	관리
reliable source	믿을 만한 소식통	sneaky bastard	사악한 녀석
come into possession	~의 소유가 되다		

Yuri, Vlad, kill them!

level C1 Scene 10 (58)

What should Olive do?

O: Don't kill us please! We should talk this over!

Game over. Try again.

O: Get your fat Russian ass back on that chair!

G: And why would I want to do that!

O: Because you're a fool if you think that you're safe. Far from it. Your precious organisation is a step away from going down the drain! But you have only yourself to blame for that! You should've found yourself a better lawyer years ago!

G: Tell me more …

ass	엉덩이
chair	의자
be a step away from	~ 직전이다
go down the drain	파산하다

Grammar explanations

간접화법: 인용어구 Reported speech: reporting words
인용어구:

what? – this ➔ that / these ➔ those

when? – yesterday ➔ the day before

where? – here ➔ there

whose? – my ➔ your, his

etc.

Olive: Count on me to unravel this mess. ➔ Olive told them to count on her to unravel that mess.　Olive: 이 엉망인 상황을 해결하기 위해서는 저를 믿어 주세요. → Olive는 그 엉망인 상황을 해결하기 위해 자신을 믿어 달라고 그들에게 말했습니다.

Brooks: I'm one of the few genuine miracle workers around here. ➔ Brooks said that he was one of the few genuine miracle workers around there.　Brooks: 저는 이곳 주변에서 진짜로 일을 잘하는 몇 안 되는 사람 중 한 명이에요. → Brook은 자신이 그곳 주변에서 진짜로 일을 잘하는 몇 안 되는 사람 중 한 명이라고 말했습니다.

Murray: He was romantically involved with my wife many years ago. ➔ Murray admitted that Willis was romantically involved with his wife many years before.　Murray: 그는 수년 전 제 아내와 연애를 하던 사이였어요. → Murray는 Willis가 수년 전 자신의 아내와 연애를 하던 사이였다는 점을 인정했습니다.

간접화법 = 새로운 관점

시간의 변화	+	인용어구의 변화
are → were, will → would etc.		this → that, ago → before etc.

level C1　Scene 10 (58)

간접화법: 명령, 제안, 요청 Reported speech: orders, suggestions and requests

단순하게 사건을 전달하는 경우	중요함이나 위급함을 표현하는 경우
주어 + 동사 + 사람 + (not) + to부정사	주어 + 동사 + that + 사람 + should (not) + 부정사
주로 사용되는 동사: say, tell, want, remind, advise, encourage, invite, promise, ask, beg, order, warn	주로 사용되는 동사: advise, command, insist, order, recommend, remind, say suggest, urge, warn

David: **I think we should call the police.** 저는 우리가 경찰에 연락해야 한다고 생각해요.

David suggests **to call** the police. ←

→ David insists **that they should** call the police. David는 그들이 경찰에 연락해야 한다고 주장했습니다.

David는 경찰에 연락할 것을 제안했습니다.

Olive: **Let me unravel this mess.** 이 엉망인 상황을 제가 해결할게요.

Olive asks **them to let** her unravel that mess. ←

→ Olive demands **that she should** unravel that mess. Olive는 그녀가 엉망인 상황을 해결하겠다고 주장했습니다.

Olive는 엉망인 상황을 자신이 해결할 수 있도록 해 달라고 그들에게 요청했습니다.

Olive: **Don't shoot, David**! 쏘지 말아요, David!

Olive ordered David **not to shoot**. ←

→ Olive ordered **that** David **should not** shoot. Olive는 David에게 총을 쏘면 안 된다고 명령했습니다.

Olive는 David에게 쏘지 말라고 명령했습니다.

동명사의 간접화법 Reported speech with gerund

동사 advise, suggest, recommend

Olive says: Gennady, you shouldn't trust Murray. ➔ OLIve recommends not trusting Murray.
Olive는 말했습니다: Gennady, Murray를 믿으면 안 돼요. → Olive는 Murray를 믿지 말라고 권고했습니다.

Olive adds: You should look for another lawyer. ➔ She suggests looking for another lawyer.
Olive는 덧붙여 말했습니다: 당신은 다른 변호사를 찾아야 해요. → 그녀는 다른 변호사를 찾을 것을 제안했습니다.

Sergey writes: Father, you should find another occupation. ➔ Sergey advises finding another occupation.
Sergey는 글을 썼습니다: 아버지, 다른 직업을 찾으셔야 해요. → Sergey는 다른 직업을 찾으라고 조언했습니다.

Sergey adds: You really should atone for all the evil things you've done. ➔ He recommends atoning for the evil Gennady has done.
Sergey는 덧붙였습니다: 당신은 당신이 저지른 모든 악행에 대해 반드시 속죄해야 해요. → 그는 Gennady에게 그가 저질은 악행에 대해 속죄할 것을 권고했습니다.

> **Remember!**
> 간접화법에서 advise, suggest와 recommend는 단순하게 동명사의 뒤에 위치할 수 있다 - 특히 사람이 아닌 행동에 중점을 둘 경우에 그러하다.

동사 + 전치사

Gennady: My son, Sergey, is in Sudan. I blame you for that! ➔ Gennady blamed Olive and David for making his son leave for Sudan.   내 아들 Sergey가 수단에 있어. 그에 대해서는 당신들에게 책임을 묻겠어! → Gennady는 그의 아들이 수단으로 떠난 책임을 Olive와 David에게 돌렸습니다.

Olive: Get your fat Russian ass back on that chair. ➔ Olive discourages Gennady from leaving so soon.   당신의 뚱뚱한 러시아 엉덩이를 다시 그 의자에 갖다 붙여요. → Olive는 Gennady가 바로 떠나는 것을 단념시켰습니다.

Olive: You're a fool if you think that you're safe. ➔ Olive accused Gennady of being a fool.   당신이 안전하다고 생각한다면 당신은 바보예요. → Olive는 Gennady의 어리석음을 비난했습니다.

> **Remember!**
> 몇몇 동사와 전치사의 조합 또한 간접화법 문장에서 사용될 수 있다. 이는 항상 동명사를 수반한다.

Communication situations

Read the following dialogues between county councillors.

Ladies and gentlemen, next on today's agenda is the memorial on the village green. We all voted in favour of one, so let us now choose who it's going to commemorate. Our Lord Bishop from the 15th century or the soldiers of World War II?

Dialogue 1

Councillor B: I know the general opinion is in favour of the soldiers but I have some objections.

Councillor A: Yes? What are they?

Councillor B: Why shall we, as a community, erect such a monument at all?

Councillor A: What do you mean?

Councillor B: There are already a number of memorials commemorating this ordeal.

Councillor A: May I just remind you that this conflict claimed the lives of over 60 million people? Are you saying that we can have too many memorials to honour them?

Councillor B: Actually, I am.

Councillor A: All right. Thank you for your input. Let's see if anyone else would like to speak now.

---

councillor 의원 | **objections** 반대 | **erect** 세우다 | **memorial** 기념비 | **ordeal** 시련 | **claim the lives** 목숨을 빼앗다 | **honour** 명예를 주다 | **input** 조언

Dialogue 2

Councillor B: We should commemorate the bishop. He was a local figure and deserves to be remembered.

Councillor A: Let me point out, however, that his attitude towards young women was controversial, to say the least.

Councillor B: How dare you! There has never been any tangible evidence against him.

Councillor A: You have to admit it's hard to rely on church papers that are over 600 years old.

Councillor B: Relying on historical statements is a standard procedure when dealing with such remote past.

Councillor A: Agreed. And it's all fine as long as the person in question is as clean as a whistle.

Councillor B: You are ready to ignore historical documents but willing to listen to historical gossip?

Councillor A: I'm just saying that we should not celebrate a person whose morality was doubtful.

Councillor B: You sound like a broken record.

Councillor A: That may be so, but I'm still right. Anyway, let's focus on the counterproposal now and see where it takes us, shall we?

---

bishop 주교 | **local figure** 지역의 인물 | **tangible evidence** 물증 | **church papers** 교회 문서 | **remote** 먼 | **Agreed.** 동의합니다. | **as clean as a whistle** 매우 깨끗한 | **ignore** 무시하다 | **be willing to** 기꺼이 ~하다 | **gossip** 소문 | **morality** 도덕성 | **doubtful** 의심스러운 | **sound like a broken record** 같은 말을 반복하다

Vocabulary plus

accusation 비난; 고발
anniversary 기념일
appeal 항소
appreciation 공감; 감사
apprehensive 걱정되는, 불안한
battle 전투
beliefs 믿음
biased 편향된
charity work 자선 사업
county 자치주
cult of personality 개인 숭배
dandelion 민들레
defend 방어하다
direct 직접적인
Disgraceful! 수치스러운
educational 교육적인
engage the audience 청중을 사로잡다
entire debate 전체인 토론
exhibition 전시회
exposed 노출된
express one's opinion 의견을 피력하다
fellow 친구
find not guilty 무죄 판결을 내리다
have a feeling ~한 예감이 들다
historical link 역사적인 관련성
I rest my case. 이상으로 마치겠습니다.

innocence 결백
intrigued 흥미로워하는
Middle Ages 중세 시대
needless to say 말할 필요도 없이
No point crying over spilt milk. 엎질러진 물이다.
opening ceremony 개회식
origin 기원, 근원
outrageous 충격적인
peasant 소작농
perch 횃대
pigeon 비둘기
poppy 양귀비
present 주다, 수여하다
rooted in ~에 원인이 있는
sham 엉터리, 가짜
share 공유하다
statue 조각상
testimony 증거
the whole of ~의 전체
vicious 잔인한
village green 마을의 중심에 있는 광장
villager 마을 사람
vital 필수적인
volunteer 자원하다
wound 부상, 상처

Cultural tips

Did you know that ...?

Counties are subnational divisions of the United Kingdom, used for the purposes of administrative, geographical and political demarcation. The names of these regions are often well known, even famous, for example: Nottinghamshire.

Scene 11 (59) — Film dialogue and vocabulary

**Read the dialogue between Beatrice (B), Murray (M) and Curtis (C).
Check the list of words and phrases below.**

B: Fear, uncertainty, confusion …

M: Beatrice, not now!

B: Should you still be hoping that everything will turn out just fine, you should know that it's a waste of time. I expect your Russian friends are already on their way. What I find particularly ironic is that you brought it on yourself. I mean Martin! Only after you had him killed did I realize how much I hate you!

M: What did you tell the Russians?

B: The Russians – nothing. They terrify me. But Olive's such a good listener. I do admire that girl! It's a pity things never worked out between her and Curtis! What I told her and what she's going to repeat to Mr Korolyov is how you've been pinching an additional share from each of the transactions you've done for them! Despite the enormous fee they've been paying you! And she'll provide enough details to prove it.

M: How do you know all this?

B: You never really minded what you said in my company or left lying on your desk for anyone to read. That must be the sole benefit of having a husband who thinks his wife is a stupid old cow. (…)

level C1

Vocabulary

fear	공포	pinch	훔치다
uncertainty	불확실함	additional	추가적인
confusion	혼란	share	공유하다
hope	바라다	despite	~에도 불구하고
ironic	아이러니한	prove	입증하다
terrify	무섭게 하다	desk	책상
listener	청자	read	읽다
admire	존경하다	benefit	장점
repeat	반복하다	stupid old cow	멍청한 여편네

What should Murray do?

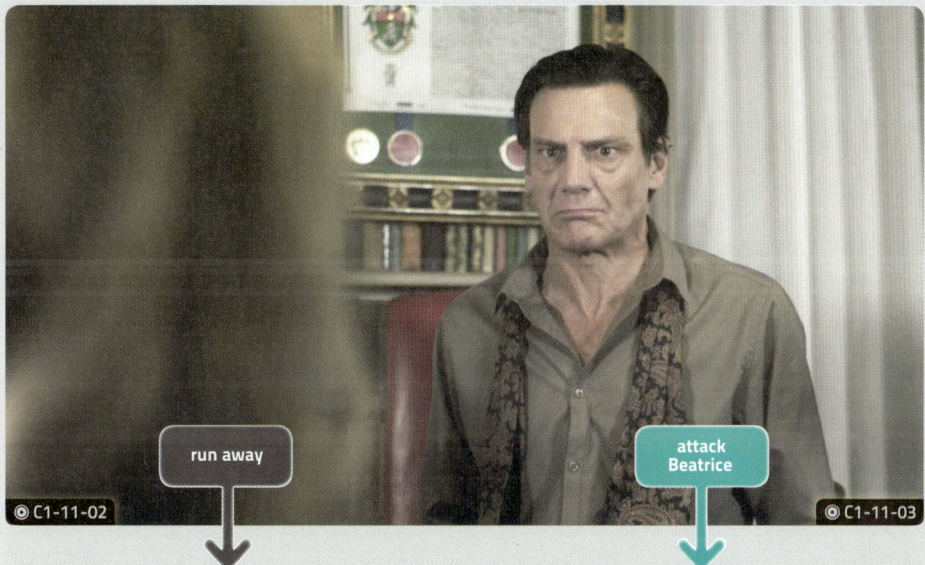

C: Dad, please stay! I'll keep you company till your friends come and pick you up!

C: Dad, don't even try! It seems you and mum are done talking. So I guess the two of us should too have a little chat before you go.

till	~까지		chat	얘기하다, 잡담하다
pickup	데리러 오다			

Grammar explanations

조건절에서의 도치 Inversion in conditional sentences
단순 조건절에서 **should**는 문장을 보다 정중하게 들리도록 하기 위해 if를 대체할 수 있다.
If you want to know the truth about Murray's fate, watch the film to the end.
→ Should you want to know the truth about Murray's fate, watch the film to the end.
머레이의 운명에 대한 진실을 알고 싶다면, 영화를 끝까지 보세요.

가정법 과거에서는 if절에서 **was/were**의 도치가 가능하다.
If I were Robert Murray, I would start looking for a remote tax paradise to move to.
→ Were I Robert Murray, I would look for a remote tax paradise to move to.
제가 Robert Murray라면, 이주하기 위해 멀리 떨어진 곳에 있는 조세피난처를 찾아볼 거예요.

가정법 과거완료에서도 보다 정중한 표현으로 만들기 위해 도치가 가능하다.
If Robert had been really clever, he would have prepared a contingency plan.
→ Had Robert been really clever, he would have prepared a contingency plan.
Robert가 정말로 영리했더라면, 그는 만일의 사태에 대한 대비를 했을 거예요.

부사구와 복문에서의 도치 Inversion with adverbials and in complex sentences

never, only, rarely 등의 부사구를 강조하기 위해서 도치가 사용될 수 있다. 아래의 패턴을 따라 해보자:

| 부사 | + | 적절한 **조동사** (do/dies, did, has/ have, can etc.) | + | 주어 | + | 동사 | + | 기타 |

I have never learnt so much in so little time.
➝ **Never have I learnt** so much in so little time.
저는 그처럼 짧은 시간에 많이 배우지 못했어요.

Robert Murray rarely makes such serious mistakes.
➝ **Rarely does Robert Murray make** such serious mistakes.
Robert Murray는 심각한 실수를 거의 저지르지 않았어요.

You shouldn't do business with the mob under any circumstances.
➝ **Under no circumstances** should you do business with the mob.
어떤 상황에서도 조직 폭력배들과 거래를 하면 안 돼요.

Robert knew little about his wife's ironic sense of humour.
➝ **Little did Robert know** about his wife's ironic sense of humour.
Robert는 아내의 아이러니컬한 유머 감각에 대해 거의 알지 못했어요.

도치는 다음과 같은 어구들로 시작하는 복문에서 종종 사용된다:
only when, only after, only by, hardly, barely, no sooner.

I realized how much I hate you **only after** you had him killed.
➝ **Only after** you had him killed **did I realize** how much I hate you!
당신이 그를 살해한 후 제가 당신을 얼마나 증오하는지 깨달았어요.

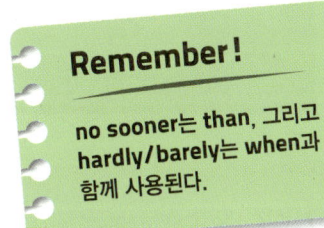

Remember!
no sooner는 than, 그리고 hardly/barely는 when과 함께 사용된다.

Olive managed to make Gennady listen to her **only by** being cheeky and decisive.
➝ **Only by** being cheeky and decisive **did Olive manage** to make Gennady listen to her.
Olive는 자신감 넘치고 결단력 있는 모습을 보임으로써 Gennady가 그녀의 말을 듣도록 만들 수 있었어요.

As soon as Alfie escaped from the garage the Russians entered.
→ **No sooner had Alfie escaped** from the garage **than** the Russians entered.
Alfie가 차고에서 도망치자마자 러시아 사람들이 들어왔어요.

Gennady had barely finished listening to Olive's explanations when he ordered his men to shoot her and David.
→ **Barely had Gennady finished** listening to Olive's explanations **when** he ordered his men to shoot her and David.
Gennady는 Olive의 설명을 다 듣자마자 부하들에게 그녀와 David에게 총을 쏘라고 명령했어요.

분열문 Cleft sentences

This film is great because it teaches and entertains at the same time.

화자가 영화에 대한 긍정적인 태도를 강조하고자 하는 경우 위 문장을 다음과 같이 바꾸어 쓸 수 있다:
What I like about this film is that it teaches and entertains at the same time.

분열문은 문장의 일부를 강조하고자 할 때 사용된다. 다양한 유형의 분열문이 존재하지만, what으로 시작하는 패턴은 보통 다음의 형식을 따른다.

| what | + | 사람 | + | like, adore, hate, prefer, need, want etc. (+전치사) | + | 목적어 | + | is / are was / were |

What I truly hate about Robert Murray is his facial expression. ← He makes really awful faces!
제가 Robert Murray에 대해 정말로 싫어하는 부분은 그의 얼굴 표정이에요. ← 그는 정말로 끔찍한 표정을 지어요.

What all of us adore about Beatrice is that she finally musters the courage to deal with her husband. ← It is a great achievement to face such a dangerous bully.
Beatrice에 대해 우리 모두가 좋아하는 부분은 그녀가 마침내 남편을 상대할 수 있는 용기를 낸다는 점이에요. ← 그처럼 위험한 악당을 상대할 수 있게 된 것은 대단한 발전이에요.

What I want to do now is watch the film again. ← It would be good for my English and it's fun!
제가 지금 바라는 것은 영화를 다시 한 번 보는 것이에요. ← 그것은 제 영어 실력에도 도움이 되고 재미도 있어요!

What the viewer should do is to learn as much as possible. ← If the viewer wants to make the most of the film, that's what he or she should do.
시청자가 해야 할 일은 가능한 많이 배우는 것이에요. ← 시청자가 영화를 최대한 이용하고 싶다면 그것이 그 혹은 그녀가 해야 하는 일이에요.

기타 분열문 형식

The thing I dislike about the film **is that** it is too short. → This is probably the only thing wrong with it for me.
그 영화에서 제가 싫어하는 점은 영화가 너무 짧다는 것이에요. → 이것이 아마도 제 마음에 들지 않는 유일한 부분일 거예요.

All I know about the set **is that** some scenes were shot in London. → That's all I know about the filming.
세트에 대해 제가 아는 것은 몇몇 장면들이 런던에서 촬영되었다는 것뿐이에요. → 영화 제작에 대해 제가 아는 것은 그것이 전부예요.

The character I like best **is** probably Beatrice. → I liked a couple of characters but I would like to emphasise who was my favourite one.
제가 가장 좋아하는 캐릭터는 Beatrice일 거예요. → 저는 두어 명의 캐릭터를 좋아하지만 가장 좋아하는 캐릭터가 누구인지 강조하고 싶어요.

The reason why I started watching the film **was** to improve my English. → I was interested in the film because I wanted to learn the language.
제가 영화 관람을 시작한 이유는 영어 실력을 향상시키기 위해서였어요. → 저는 언어를 배우고 싶었기 때문에 영화에 흥미를 느꼈어요.

Communication situations

Read the following dialogues between students who are also flatmates. Check the list of words and phrases below.

Hi, how was your day at uni today? Oh, before you answer. Sorry for the mess, I know it's my turn this week but ... Could you do the housework for me? Please.

Dialogue 1

Student B: Well, I'm not happy about that but OK. As long as you take one extra week of cleaning soon.

Student A: Deal! And I'm really sorry. I have no choice, I have to finish this today.

Student B: A deal is a deal, remember. What's giving you so much trouble?

Student A: Well, I'm trying to write a book review here.

Student B: I see. Then if you need proofreading, I'd be happy to have a look at your text later.

Student A: You would? That's great! One problem solved.

housework 집안일 | proofreading 검토 | review 후기 | uni 대학

Dialogue 2

Student B: I did your work last week. Sorry, I've got some things to do, too.

Student A: Well, I'm trying to write a book review here.

Student B: Yes, I remember now. A sample review for the literary blog, right?

Student A: Exactly.

Student B: You'll be fine. Just remember to stick to the golden blogging rules.

Student A: Which are?

Student B: Reading online is like flicking through photos.

Student A: I'm not following you.

Student B: Short text, concise paragraphs and a witty headline.

Student A: I'm writing an intelligent review, not some "attention grabber" for a tabloid. Kindly keep your recipes for mass-produced spam to yourself.

---

concise 간결한 | **flick through** 획획 넘기다 | **give trouble** 애먹이다 | **headline** 헤드라인 | **intelligent** 지적인 | **kindly** 친절하게 | **literary blog** 문학 관련 블로그 | **paragraph** 문단, 단락 | **sample** 견본, 샘플 | **witty** 재치 있는

Dialogue 3

Student B: Yeah, OK. I've seen you working a lot recently. By the way, what are you working on?

Student A: A book review. But to tell you the truth, my heart's not in this kind of journalism.

Student B: Stop complaining and take the bull by the horns.

Student A: Yeah, well ... It's all in the very early stages yet. Or, to be honest: I don't know where to start.

Student B: Think about the style. Once you hook the reader with the opening sentence, keep the tension or humour going.

Student A: That's all very well and good, but how do I start? Great opening sentences don't grow on trees, you know.

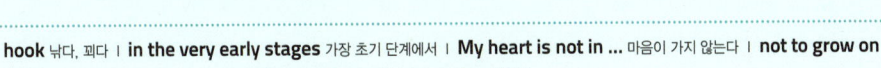

hook 낚다, 꿰다 | **in the very early stages** 가장 초기 단계에서 | **My heart is not in ...** 마음이 가지 않는다 | **not to grow on trees** 그냥 얻어지는 것이 아니다 | **opening sentence** 서문 | **tension** 긴장감

Vocabulary plus

accuracy 정확성

Blast! 제기랄!

Can I tempt you? 먹어 볼래?

coherent 일관성 있는, 논리정연한

colloquial 구어체의

common thread 공통된 맥락

contribution 공헌

convey 전달하다

corresponding 비슷한

craft 공예; 기술

dead end 막다른 길

draft 초안, 원고

faculty 학부

fame 명성

Fear doubles all. 두려움은 모든 것을 배가시킨다.

food for thought 깊이 생각할 거리

genre 장르

give away 주다

It gives you credit. 그것은 당신에게 신뢰감을 준다.

journalist 저널리스트, 기자

literacy 읽고 쓸 수 있는 능력

notion 개념, 관념

plotless 줄거리 없는

prior preparation 사전 준비

regardless of ~에 상관없이

self-importance 자존, 자만

set down ~을 적어 두다

stuff it 뭐 어때

views 견해

well-defined 명확한

Cultural tips

Did you know that ...?

There are newspapers distributed nationally in the UK, and others serving only a region or local area. National daily newspapers publish on every day except 25th December and on Sundays. There are also Sunday newspapers. UK newspapers can generally be split into two distinct categories: broadsheets and tabloids. The more serious and intellectual newspapers, usually referred to as "the quality press" or "broadsheets" (due to their large size), focus on political reporting or overseas news. The others, generally referred to as "tabloids" or "popular press", tend to focus more on celebrity coverage and other human interest stories.

Scene 12 (60)   Film dialogue and vocabulary

Read Olive's monologue. Check the list of words and phrases below.

> Being a reasonable man, Gennady let himself be convinced that what I'd learnt from Beatrice was enough to destroy him, should I wish so ... So he let us live.

Then we let the French out. Cloutier was still brooding over my past "transgressions" ...

But I talked sense into him and he won't be bothering me again. Rumour has it that he and Alfie ...

Started working together in the art business. Who would've thought it, huh?

We returned to Old Berry so that I can recover from my injury and ... get my priorities right.

I haven't stolen anything in two months. Do I miss it? No! Yes! Sometimes!

As for Murray ... Having left the Manor, he vanished mysteriously.

Nobody misses him anyway. Beatrice has reclaimed her property. She and Curtis are doing all right.

My relationship with David is a healthy one. We've actually been thinking about ...

Vocabulary

convince	확신시키다	get one's priorities right	무엇이 가장 중요한지 판단을 하고 행동하다
brood over	~에 대해 골똘히 생각하다	vanish	사라지다
transgression	위반	mysteriously	묘연하게
talk sense into	~에게 알아 듣게 이야기하다	nobody	아무도 ~않다
Rumour has it ...	소문에 따르면	reclaim	되찾다
recover (from)	~에서 회복하다		

Grammar explanations

분사구문 Participle clauses
분사구문은 새로운 정보를 전달하는데, while/when 절뿐만 아니라 관계사절을 대체한다.

과거분사 Past participle 수동의 의미를 표현할 때 사용

Robert Murray, **who was blinded by greed**, stole more and more from the Russians.
→ **Blinded by greed**, Murray stole more and more from the Russians.
Robert Murray는, 탐욕에 눈이 멀어서, 러시아 사람들로부터 점점 더 많은 것을 훔쳤습니다. → 탐욕에 눈이 멀어서 Murray는 러시아 사람들로부터 점점 더 많은 것을 훔쳤습니다.

Allen Adams, **whom everybody forgot**, led an unfortunate life as an old drunk.
→ **Forgotten by everybody**, Allen Adams led an unfortunate life as an old drunk.
Allen Adams는, 모두가 잊고 있었는데, 늙은 술꾼으로 불행한 삶을 살았습니다. → 모두에게서 잊힌 Allen은 늙은 술꾼으로 불행한 삶을 살았습니다.

The old painting, **which was highly prized by art experts**, happened to be a part of Murray's collection. → **Highly prized by art experts**, the old painting happened to be a part of Murray's collection.
그 오래된 그림은, 미술 전문가들에 의해 높이 평가되었는데, Murray의 수집품의 일부가 되었습니다. → 미술 전문가들에 의해 높이 평가되었던 그 오래된 그림은 Murray의 수집품의 일부가 되었습니다.

현재분사 Present Participle 능동의 의미를 표현할 때 사용

Gennady, **who was a reasonable man**, let himself be convinced. → **Being a reasonable man**, Gennady let himself be convinced.
Gennady는, 이성적인 사람이었는데, 스스로를 납득시켰습니다. → 이성적인 사람이었던 Gennady는 스스로를 납득시켰습니다.

David, **who was working as a small town police officer**, never expected so many dramatic adventures. → **Working as a small town police officer**, David never expected so many dramatic adventures.
David는, 작은 마을의 경찰관으로 일하고 있었는데, 그처럼 많은 극적인 모험을 결코 예상하지 못했습니다. → 작은 마을의 경찰관으로 일하고 있던 David는 그처럼 많은 극적인 모험을 결코 예상하지 못했습니다.

Gennady learnt the truth about Murray **while he was trying to eliminate Murray's enemies**. → Gennady learnt the truth about Murray **trying to eliminate Murray's enemies**.
Gennady는 Murray의 적들을 제거하려고 노력하는 동안 Murray에 관한 진실을 알게 되었습니다. → Gennady는 Murray의 적들을 제거하려고 노력하는 동안 Murray에 관한 진실을 알게 되었습니다.

완료 분사(*having done*)를 포함한 절은 다른 행동보다 앞서 발생한 행동을 언급할 때 사용된다. 이는 주로 as/after로 시작하는 시간의 부사절을 대체하며, 과거형이나 과거완료를 대체할 수도 있다.

After Murray **had left** the Manor, he vanished mysteriously.
→ Having left **the Manor**, Murray vanished mysteriously.
Murray는 저택을 떠난 후 수수께끼처럼 사라졌습니다.

Alfie **worked for many years** as a mechanic, **but then** he was hired by an art dealer.
→ Having worked as a mechanic for many years, Alfie was hired by an art dealer.
Alfie는 정비사로서 수 년간 일을 했지만 미술품 중개인으로 채용되었습니다.

Sergey **graduated** from hydrology at Oxford and started working in Sudan.
→ Having graduated **from Oxford**, Sergey started working in Sudan.
Sergey는 옥스포드에서 수문학과를 졸업하고 수단에서 일을 시작했습니다.

Communication situations

Read the following dialogues between a mother and a daughter talking about the plans for the future.

Sweetie, I'm glad we've finally gone out together. We should do it more often, don't you think? Now, there is one thing we have to talk about. What are your plans for the future?

Dialogue 1

Daughter: I'd like to continue my blog.

Mother: OK. I can see you are really into it and I'm glad. But I'm asking seriously.

Daughter: But mum, I am taking it seriously.

Mother: What about your studies? Or some work at least?

Daughter: Mum, I can start my studies whenever I want.

Mother: That's true, but the later you start the more difficult it is to make it to the end.

Daughter: I don't agree, mum.

Mother: You don't?

Daughter: No, there is The Open University. I can get my Bachelor's, or even Master's, online.

Mother: Really? So maybe I could enroll? I've always wanted to study the history of art.

Daughter: Yeah, go for it, mum!

Mother: Thanks, sweetie! But aren't we supposed to be talking about you?

---

enroll 등록하다 | sweetie 사랑스러운 사람을 부르는 말

Dialogue 2

Daughter: To be honest I feel I'm in a fix.
Mother: Why is that? What's the problem?
Daughter: I'm tired of school and this everyday routine.
Mother: But that's life, love.
Daughter: But I can't feel like that when I'm barely 20.
Mother: Then find a way to change it.
Daughter: Yes, I've been thinking about it a lot recently.
Mother: Have you got something in mind?
Daughter: I thought about working a bit to save some money for a trip.
Mother: Where would you like to go?
Daughter: The first six months, to South America, and for the second half of the year, to Alaska.
Mother: A year of travelling. That's pretty long. You may have difficulties coming back to the daily grind.

be in a fix 정체기에 있다 | **daily grind** 매일 반복되는 지루한 일

Dialogue 3

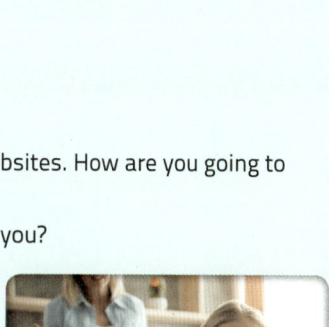

Mother: Oh love, I think you've read too many gossip websites. How are you going to become a celebrity?
Daughter: Really, you have no idea about social media, do you?
Mother: That's correct, I don't.
Daughter: I'm not going to be a celebrity.
Mother: So are you going to run your blog just for fun?
Daughter: Is there something wrong with that?
Mother: And what about the money, love?
Daughter: Believe me, there is some good money in that business.
Mother: OK, but how are you going to make it?
Daughter: Trust me, I know how social media work.
Mother: I just have to believe in you more, don't I? Well, there's no time like the present.

celebrity 유명인사

Vocabulary plus

airy-fairy 비현실적인, 애매한

by no means 대단한

combine 결합하다

creative 창조적인

depress 우울하게 만들다

designer 디자이너

discover 발견하다

doer 행동가, 실천가

egghead 지식인

follow the beaten track 관례대로 하다

gap year 갭이어(고교 졸업 후 대학에 진학하기 전에 1년 동안 갖는 기간)

independent 독립적인

just round the corner 곧

major 전공

mature 성인이 된

part-time job 시간제 근무

practice 실제

practise 연습하다

pragmatist 실용주의자

proud 자랑스러워하는

relate 관련시키다

settle into a routine 일상으로 자리 잡다

theoretical knowledge 이론적 지식

theorist 이론가

Cultural tips

Did you know that ...?

Established in 1969, the Open University (OU) is a public distance learning and research university. The majority of its students are based in the UK and mainly study offcampus. Many of its courses (both undergraduate and postgraduate) can also be studied anywhere in the world.

Translation 해석

Scene 1 (49)

Film dialogue and vocabulary p. 8~9

B: 쯧쯧… 자네 강아지가 심하게 다쳤군.
B: 봐, 어깨에 예쁜 총상을 입었어! 난리가 났겠네! 그리고 등에는 엄청난 자상도 있고! 코 수술도 했네… 심하게 부러져서 똑바로 세웠어. 솜씨가 좋군… 아이고! 다시 예쁘게 하느라 돈을 엄청 썼구먼.
D: 이렇게 피 흘리다간 죽겠어요! 당장 치료해 주시겠어요?
B: 그건 자네한테 달렸네. 내 서비스가 좀 비싸거든! (…) 좋아! 좋아! 이 정도 돈이면, 수술도 해주고 시체 처리도 해주지. 결과가 만족스럽지 못할 경우 말이야!
D: 시체 처리? 살릴 수 있어요? 없어요?
B: 최선을 다하겠네! 이 아가씨한테 필요한 건 기적이야. 하지만 자네가 운이 좋군. 나야말로 이 동네에 몇 안 되는 진짜 기적의 손이거든. 시작할까?

refuse
D: 아뇨, 진짜 병원으로 데려갈 거예요.

agree
D: 하세요!
B: 좋아! 날 좀 도와줘야 하니까 깨끗한 앞치마 두르고 손도 깨끗하게 씻어. 걱정하지 마! 당신 강아지는 곧 원반 놀이를 하게 될 테니까! 충고하는데… 마취제를 주사했지만 내가 쓰는 건 병원에서 쓰는 것과는 비교가 안 돼. 소리 지르고 발악하거든, 꽉 잡고 그냥 버텨! 알았지?

Communication situations p. 12~13

Man: 실례합니다, 부인, 괜찮으신가요?

Dialogue 1
Woman: 잘 모르겠어요. 제가 왜 잔디밭에 앉아 있죠?
Man: 정신을 잃으셨던 것 같아요. 아픈 곳이 있나요?
Woman: 아니요, 하지만 당신이 그다지 잘 보이지 않고 당신 목소리도 겨우 들을 수 있어요.
Man: 제 손가락이 움직이는 것을 볼 수 있나요?
Woman: 죄송해요. 한 번 더 해 주시겠어요?
Man: 부인, 머리에 큰 충격을 받으신 것 같군요. 구급대를 불러야 할 것 같아요.

Woman: 그렇게 해 주세요. 저의 상태를 제 아들에게도 알려 주실 수 있으신가요?

Man: 네, 물론이죠. 번호가 어디에 있나요?

Woman: 제 전화기에 긴급 전화번호로 있어요.

Man: 알겠습니다. 찾았어요. 즉시 아드님에게 전화할게요.

Dialogue 2

Woman: 잘 모르겠어요.

Man: 일어날 수 있겠어요?

Woman: 오 아니요, 그럴 수 없어요. 내 다리!

Man: 제가 볼게요. 음, 좋아 보이지는 않네요. 아픈가요?

Woman: 지금 보고 있는데, 정말로 아파요.

Man: 놀랍지는 않군요, 전체가 피와 멍으로 덮여 있으니. 당신 발로 일어서실 수 있겠어요?

Woman: 아니요, 너무 아파요.

Man: 흠, 골절되었을 수도 있겠네요. 구급대가 올 때까지 고정시켜 볼게요.

Woman: 안 돼요, 만지지 마세요.

Man: 그래요. 좋아요, 그럼 만지지 않을게요. 제가 구급차를 부르는 동안 움직이지 말고 그대로 계세요.

Dialogue 3

Woman: 왜요? 제가 아파 보이나요?

Man: 음, 얼굴 전체가 빨갛게 보여서요.

Woman: 맞아요. 제가 벌에 쏘여서 지금 알레르기 반응이 나타나고 있는 거예요.

Man: 그리고 부어 있어요. 침을 삼키실 수 있나요?

Woman: 네, 방금 항히스타민제를 먹었어요.

Man: 오, 잘했군요. 그러면 이제 곧 효과가 나타나겠네요.

Woman: 네. 이번이 처음은 아니니 걱정하지 마세요.

Man: 그렇다면 되었어요. 안녕히 계세요.

Scene 2 (50)

Film dialogue and vocabulary   p. 16~17

O: 일어나! 일어나, 이 배신자야!

O: 나쁜 자식! 당신 때문에 내가 어떤 위험에 빠졌는지 알기나 해!

D: 뭐라고요? 내가 당신 목숨을 구했어요, 안 그래요? 당신도 날 구해줬지만 내가 안 갔으면…

D: 서류를 나한테 가져왔어야죠. 내가 직접 해결했을 거예요!

D: 그래요? 머리와 부하들을 혼자서 어떻게 상대할 건데요?

O: 방법을 찾았을 거예요! 협박한다든가… 뭔가 숨기고 있어요. 틀림없어요! 그 정보를 이용할 수만 있다면… 하지만 당신이 폴더를 넘겨주는 바람에… 그게 뭐예요?

D: 폴더에서 빼냈는데… 글쎄요… 필요하면 머리를 협박하려고요?

O: 제법이네요, 오언 순경님. 이제 이 디스크를 해킹할 방법을 찾아야 해요!

let Olive do it

D: 난 이런 건 전혀 몰라요! (…) 선생님! 도와주세요!

make a suggestion

D: 나한테 맡겨요, 알았죠?

O: 어떻게 할 생각이에요?

D: 런던에 아는 친구가 있는데 온갖 기계를 잘 다루고 기술에 꽤 빠삭한 거 같아요!

O: 설마… 젠장 걔는 안 돼요!

A: 데이비드, 친구! 이렇게 반가울 수가!

Communication situations   p. 20~22

Gennady: 모두들 안녕하신가.

Dialogue 1

Gangster: 안녕하세요, 게다니, 함께해 줘서 고마워요. 무언가 마시겠어요?

Gennady: 커피가 좋겠군. 자, 사업 이야기를 시작하지.

Gangster: 아시다시피, 우리는 사업을 확장해야 합니다.

Gennady: 그래, 무슨 말인지 알겠군. 개인적으로 나는 합법적인 일을 좋아하지. 우리는 부동산 시장에 초점을 맞춰야 해.

Gangster: 훌륭한 사람들은 생각이 같군요.

Gennady: 문제가 될 것으로 보이는 것은 대출 정책이야. 금융 위기 이후에 은행들이 더 이상 예전처럼 관대하지가 않아. 구입 자금을 마련할 수 있는 다른 방법을 찾아내야 해.

Gangster: 그건 제게 맡겨 두시죠.

Gennady: 그래. 좋아.

Dialogue 2

Gangster: 기분이 언짢으신 것 같습니다.

Gennady: 맞아, 그래. 하지만 신경 쓰지 마. 계속 얘기해봐.

Gangster: 이번 모임의 주된 이유는 새로운 시장으로의 진입에 대해 생각해 보아야 한다는 점 때문입니다.

Gennady: 더 자세히 말해 주겠나? 국내 시장인가, 아니면 해외 시장인가?

Gangster: 국내 시장을 고려해 보도록 하죠.

Gennady: 그래, 무슨 말인지 알겠어. 개인적으로 나는 합법적인 일을 좋아하지. 우리는 부동산 시장에 초점을 맞춰야 해.

Gangster: 저는 잘 모르겠군요.

Gennady: 왜? 이 시장에 문제라도 있나? 몇 년 동안 꽤 안정적이었고, 안전하고, 돈도 충분해. 식은 죽 먹기라고 말하고 싶군.

Gangster: 모스크바에 있는 본사와 상의해 보는 것이 어떨까요? 그에 관해 그들이 해 줄 말이 있지 않을까요?

Gennady: 일리 있는 말이군. 오늘 그들에게 연락해 볼게. 지금만큼 좋은 때란 없지.

Gangster: 제게도 알려 주세요.

Dialogue 3

Ganster: 전체적으로 말하자면, 저는 사업을 전방위로 확장하고 싶어요.

Gennady: 내가 제대로 이해했다면 해외 진출을 원하는 것이로군.

Ganster: 제 말이 바로 그거예요.

Gennady: 계속 얘기해봐.

Ganster: 저는 부동산 시장을 생각했어요. - 여느 때와는 다르게 합법적인 사업이죠. 이미 몇 번의 조사를 해 두었고요.

Gennady: 전망이 밝아 보이는군. 수치들을 내가 한 번 보도록 하지.

Dialogue 4

Gangster: 그러면 우리가 무엇을 해야 하나요?

Gennady: 음, 우리는 자산 포트폴리오를 만들어서 자산을 임대할 수 있어. 사고 파는 대신에.

Gangster: 남부 유럽은 최고의 휴양지예요.

Gennady: 자네에게 무슨 문제라도 있나? 그거 농담이야?

Scene 3 (51)

Film dialogue and vocabulary   p. 24~27

M: 시체로 발견됐다니! 살해된 겁니까?

P: 네.

P: 물론, 선생님과 세부사항을 공유할 순 없습니다. 현재 조사 중인 사건이니까요. 하지만 선생님의 직원들이 범행에 연루된 것 같습니다. 현장에서 상당량의 약물이 발견됐습니다!

M: 마약요?

P: 네. 머리 씨, 알고 계셨습니까? 선생님의 보안 요원 중 일부가 전과가 아주 화려하던데요. 고용하기 전에 확인하셨을 거 아닙니까?

M: 아뇨, 안 했습니다. 내 친구가 추천한 사람들이었습니다. 친구가 자질을 높이 평가하기에 난 그 말을 믿었죠. 그렇게 쉽게 믿는 게 아니었는데요, 그렇죠?

P: 그들 중 누가 마약 하는 걸 본 적 있습니까?

M: 네, 사실, 조시에게 정식으로 항의했었죠. 조시는 팀장이었습니다.

P: 조슈아 올던 말씀입니까?

M: 네! 말했듯이, 정식으로 항의했습니다. 제가 들은 바로는 조시와 팀원들이 근무 중에 마리화나를 했다고 하더군요. 어쨌든 그들을 곧 해고했을 겁니다.

P: 그렇군요… 마틴 윌리스라는 남자를 아십니까? 나이는 50세. 런던의 개인 투자가입니다.

`tell the truth`

M: 네, 압니다! 윌리스는… 내 아내와 사랑하는 사이였죠. 오래전에요. 그는 실연의 상처를 극복하지 못했어요! 그 사람은 왜요?

P: 이상하게도 그 사람의 시신도 현장에서 발견됐습니다. 그의 지갑에서 사모님의 사진이 나왔죠. 확실하지는 않지만 그와 보안 요원들이 선생님에 대한 음모를 꾸몄을 수도 있습니다. 저희가 그 가능성도 조사할 겁니다! 협조해 주셔서 감사합니다.

`lie`

M: 아뇨, 마틴 윌리스라는 사람은 모르는데요.

P: 이상하군요. 그가 사모님을 속속들이 알았다고 믿을 만한 근거가 있습니다. 선생님한테도 관심이 많았고요. 머리 씨, 곧 다시 뵙게 될 겁니다.

B: 마틴 윌리스한테 무슨 일이 생긴 거죠?

Communication situations   p. 30~31

Officer: 안녕하세요, 런던 경찰서의 존슨 경찰관입니다. 어떻게 도와 드릴까요?

`Dialogue 1`

Caller: 자동차 충돌 사고를 신고하려고 전화했어요.

Officer: 구급차나 소방대가 필요하신가요?

Caller: 네. 네 대의 차량이 충돌을 해서 누군가가 다쳤을 수도 있어요.

Officer: 좋습니다. 장소가 어디죠?

Caller: 처음에는 M25에 있었고, 그 다음에는 A225, 지금은 다트퍼드로 빠지는 출구에 있어요.

Officer: 그러시군요. 사고는 이미 저희 시스템에 입력해 두었습니다. 긴급 구조대가 가고 있는 중이에요. 당신 차에 있는 사람이나 당신에게 개별적인 도움이 필요한가요?

Caller: 구조에 몇 시간 정도 걸린다면, 따뜻한 음료가 필요할 것 같아요.

Officer: 좋습니다. 자세한 내용을 듣기에 앞서, 차에 아이들이 있나요?

Caller: 네, 둘이요. 한 살짜리와 일곱 살짜리죠.

Officer: 아기가 분유를 먹나요, 아니면 모유를 먹나요?

Caller: 때에 따라 달라요. 다섯 시간 후에는 분유가 필요할 거예요.

Officer: 그렇군요. 알겠습니다. 이제 자세한 내용을 알려 주세요.

Dialogue 2

Caller: 방화를 신고하려고 전화했어요.

Officer: 목격자이신가요, 아니면 방화의 피해자신가요?

Caller: 음, 저는 괜찮은데, 불이 제 재산에 영향을 끼쳤어요.

Officer: 그렇군요. 무엇이 영향을 받았나요?

Caller: 제 차요.

Officer: 알겠습니다. 언제 발생했나요?

Caller: 잘 모르겠어요. 화요일 이후로 제가 집에 없었거든요.

Officer: 좋습니다. 경찰관이 지금 가고 있는 중입니다. 자세한 내용을 알려 주시겠어요?

Dialogue 3

Caller: 자동차 충돌 사고를 신고하려고 전화했어요.

Officer: 구급차나 소방대가 필요하신가요?

Caller: 저는 괜찮은데 다른 운전자가 피를 흘리고 있는 것 같아요.

Officer: 그렇군요, 구급차가 가고 있는 중입니다. 충돌 사고에 대해 자세한 내용을 말씀해 주실 수 있으신가요? 몇 대의 차량이 관련되어 있죠?

Caller: 두 대요: 트럭 한 대와 제 차예요.

Officer: 좋습니다. 충돌 사고는 어디에서 발생했나요?

Caller: 저희는 커네리 워프 역으로부터 50미터 떨어진 곳에 있어요.

Officer: 알겠습니다. 충돌 사고로 교통이 막혔나요?

Caller: 네, 안타깝지만 저희가 교차로 전체를 막고 있어요.

Officer: 그렇군요. 차에 그대로 계시면서 경찰을 기다려 주십시오.

Scene 4 (52)

Film dialogue and vocabulary   p. 34~36

B: 시체로 발견돼요? 조시와 다른 요원들과 함께요?

B: 당신이 죽이라고 시켰어요?

M: 터무니없군! 누가 그랬는지 나도 몰라!

B: 당신이잖아!

`attack Beatrice`

M: 오늘도 또 "이상한 날들" 중 하루인가, 베아트리스? 약의 유혹을 못 견디겠지, 안 그래? 그 미친놈은 내가 안 죽였어! 제발 내 탓 좀 그만해! 특히 당신이 그 꼴로 사는 게! 그만 내 앞에서 꺼져!

B: (…) 경찰이죠? 올드 베리의 캠벨 저택에 사는 베아트리스 머리라고 합니다. 제 남편에 관해 신고할 게 있어요… 로버트 머리요.

`deny`

M: 내가 안 죽였어! 여보, 그 집착증 미치광이가 몇 년 동안 우리 인생에 끼어들었어! 우릴 파멸시킬 음모를 꾸미고, 우리가 믿는 사람들로부터 정보를 사들이고, 우리를 무너트릴 비리를 파고 다녔지…

B: 아주 많이 찾았겠죠, 안 그래요?

M: 뭘?

B: 비리요… 이 집에 아주 많잖아요. 그가 당신의 불륜을 폭로했더라도 소용이 없었겠죠, 안 그래요? 당신의 명성에 약간 금이 갔겠지만, 크게 걱정할 거리는 못 됐겠죠! 하지만 그가 사람들에게 폭로하려던 게 당신이 처리한 거래들이었다면… 당신이 공공연하게 떠드는 거래들 말고… 진짜 거액이 관련된 거래들 말이에요. 무시무시한 남자들과 한 거래들요. 차가운 눈에 외국인 억양을 가진 남자들요. 궁금하네요… 경찰이 그 거래들에 관심을 가질지 궁금해요.

M: 공허한 말뿐이야, 베아트리스. 당신은 말은 거창한데 행동은 못 하지. 당신 인생이 시궁창 같은 진짜 이유가 그거야!

Communication situations   p. 38~39

Host: 안녕하세요, 자기 계발에 관한 저희 주간 팟캐스트를 찾아 주셔서 고맙습니다. 오늘은 일상 생활에서 접할 수 있는 다양한 종류의 기다림에 대처하는 방법에 관한 이야기를 해 보겠습니다.

Guest: 매우 힘든 상황인데 어쩔 수 없이 기다려야 하는 때가 특히 그렇죠.

Host: 맞습니다. 그리고 힘들어하는 사람에게는 종종 아무런 도움도 주어지지 않죠. 사람들은 "긍정적으로 생각해라."는 말만 계속할 뿐이에요.

Guest: 음, 문제의 핵심은 "긍정적인 것"이 반드시 "기쁨"이나 "즐거움"을 의미하지는 않는다는 거예요.

Host: 정확히 그렇습니다. 저는 대부분의 심리학자, 종교적 권위, 그리고 부모들이 성장에는 고통이 따른다는 말에 동의한다고 생각해요.

Guest: 정말 그래요. 심지어 "성장통"이라는 이야기도 하잖아요, 그렇지 않나요?

Host: 맞습니다. 고통과 변화를 두려워해서는 안 됩니다. 하지만 문제에 보다 잘 대처하기 위해서는 어떤 건설적인 전략을 세울 수 있을까요?

Guest: 건전한 대처 방안 중 하나는 우리가 견뎌야 하는 기다림을 모두 포용하는 것이 될 거예요.

Host: 정확히 어떤 말씀이시죠? 그러한 환경에서 우리에게 도움이 될 행동에 관한 사례를 찾을 수 있을까요?

Guest: 음, 우리는 통상적으로 괴롭고 혼란스러울 때 해답을 필요로 해요.

Host: 우선 그러한 점이 질문을 공식화하는 것과 관련이 있을 것 같아요.

Guest: 그렇기도 하고 아니기도 하죠. 몇몇 질문들은 다른 질문보다 유용한 경향이 있어요.

Host: 무슨 말씀이신가요? 그러면 우리 자신에게 어떤 질문을 하는 것이 좋다고 생각하시나요?

Guest: "왜 나는 안 되지"라고 물을 수도 있을 거예요. 하지만 정말로 좋은 질문은 "그것으로부터 내가 무엇을 배울 수 있을까?"예요.

Host: 그러면 자책을 하거나 보다 큰 그림에 집중하던가 둘 중 하나를 택할 수 있군요. 두 가지 옵션 모두 고통스럽겠지만, 장기적으로 보면 후자가 더 생산적으로 보여요.

Scene 5 (53)

Film dialogue and vocabulary   p. 42~44

A: 불쌍한 올리브, 대체 무슨 일에 말려든 거야? 총질하는 게 네 취향은 아니었잖아.

O: 네 도움이 필요해!

A: 당연하지! 저 친구를 보는 순간 이렇게 될 줄 알았어. 나쁜 영향을 주는 친구야! 내가 네 곁을 지켰다면, 이런 비참한 꼴은 안 봤을 거야!

O: 넌 내 편이었던 적이 없어. 내 지갑 주변을 맴돌았을 뿐이지.

A: 어떻게 그런 말을 할 수 있어? 우리 사이의 특별한 관계는 돈을 뛰어넘는 거야! 알았어! 무슨 일이고 얼마 줄 건데?

D: 돈은 안 줘! 그냥 하는 거야!

A: 웃기시네!

`make a threat`
D: 올리브, 이 친구가 생각할 시간이 필요한 것 같아요! 창고에 며칠 더 가둬두는 게 어떨까요?

A: 그러시든가! 썩은 음식 먹고 배설물 넘실대는 양동이 옆에서 자는 게 너무 좋더라. 그 프랑스인과 같이 있는 것도… 환상적이야! 빨리 안 가?

`bribe Alfie`
D: 좋아! 30% 주지.

A: 얼마의 30%?

O: 데이비드, 저 인간한테는 10%도 과분해요!

A: 30% 밑으로는 절대 안 돼! 그래서 그게 얼만데?

D: 어림잡아서… 50만 파운드!

A: 50만 파운드! 너와 이 부패 경찰이 큰 건수 잡았을 줄 알았어!

A: 내가 뭘 하면 되는데?

O: 일단은 여기에 어떤 추악한 비밀이 숨겨져 있는지 알아내!

Communication situations   p. 46

A: 소셜 캠페인용 신규 프로젝트 신청서를 살펴보았나요? 그 모든 것에 대한 자금을 마련할 수 없어서 정말 안타까워요.

Dialogue 1
B: 그건 사실이지만, 여기에 정말로 제 시선을 사로잡는 것이 있어요.
A: 음, 지금 살펴보는 것이 어떨까요?
B: 유전자 변형 식품과 관련된 캠페인이 유망해 보여요.
A: 하지만 그에 대해 찬성하고 싶으신가요, 아니면 반대하고 싶으신가요?
B: 음, 찬성하는 그룹은 우리가 그들을 찬성하는 캠페인을 기획한다면 우리에게 상당한 금액을 기부하겠다고 약속했어요.
A: 뭐라고요? 언제부터 우리가 뇌물에 근거해서 캠페인을 선정했죠?

Dialogue 2
B: 제가 당신 말을 제대로 이해했는지 잘 모르겠군요. 모든 소셜 캠페인은 적극적인 것이에요. 그것은 당연한 거예요.
A: 물론 그렇지만, 우리가 초점을 맞추는 모든 이슈가 반드시 고통스러운 것일 필요는 없어요.
B: 왜 그렇게 된 거죠? 사람들을 불편하게 만드는 것이 사실상 우리의 업무라는 것을 알고 있는 건가요?
A: 더 이상 폭력적인 것과 비극적인 것들을 모두 받아들일 수는 없어요.
B: 좋아요, 힘들 수 있다는 점은 알지만, 흥분하지는 말도록 하죠. 우리가 하는 일이 중요해요.

Scene 6 (54)

Film dialogue and vocabulary   p. 50~52

M: 일을 좀 더 똑똑하게 처리할 줄 알았네!
M: 시체들을 없애버렸어야지! 어떻게 했지? 코카인을 심어놔? 이제 내 직원들이 마약 밀매 혐의를 받고 있어! 이래서야 내가 어떻게 조용하게 움직이나?
G: 시간이 너무 촉박했어! 경찰들이 코앞에 닥쳤고 마침 녀석들 차에 코카인이 있더군! 자… 말해봐… 상황이 얼마나 엿 같은 거지?
M: 이미 경찰관이 다녀갔어. 나한테 묻더군…
G: 내가 물었잖아. "상황이 얼마나 엿 같은 거지?"
M: 디스크에 우리 초창기 관계에 대한 일부 기록이 있어. 당신이 여기서 하는 일을 연막 치려고 세운 위장 회사와 관계된 거지. 하지만 장담하는데, 우리가 작업한 돈세탁에 관한 기록은… 들어있지 않아!

G: 이해가 안 되는군! 내가 위험한 건가? 아닌가?

> be arrogant

M: 당신이 내 신변 보호를 위해 얼마나 노력하냐에 달렸지! 이해하겠나, 러시아 친구?

> be cooperative

M: 우리 둘 다 위험해. 하지만 우리가 힘을 합치면 해결할 수 있어. 게나디, 우리가 거래한 지 20년이 넘었어! 우린 친구라고, 젠장! 같이 머리를 맞대고, 이 일을 처리할 방법을 찾은 다음 다시 돈을 버는 거야!

G: 그 말이 맞을지도 몰라! 그럼, 확실한 방법은 다 죽이는 거야. 관련됐거나 관련됐을지 모르는 사람 전부 다, 그 여자, 그 남자 친구, 그 주변인, 전부.

M: 그래, 전부 다! …그리고 앨런 애덤스도!

G: 누구? (…)

A: 올리브, 앨런 애덤스라는 이름 들어봤어?

Communication situations   p. 55~57

Husband: 현실을 직시해야 해. 나는 일자리를 잃었어. 우리가 월 예산을 확보하기 위해서는 소비를 줄여야만 해.

Dialogue 1

Wife: 여보, 너무 비관적으로 생각하지는 마. 당신은 분명 곧 다른 일자리를 찾게 될 거야.

Husband: 여보, 현실적이 되어야 해. 노동 시장은 핵심 고객 관리자들로 가득하다고. 불가능하다고 말하는 것은 아니지만 동일한 근무 조건을 가진 일자리를 찾는 건 분명 쉽지 않을 거야.

Wife: 우리의 생활 수준이 낮아질 수도 있다고 말하는 거야?

Husband: 그것이 바로 내가 말하고 있는 바야.

Wife: 좋아! 주변 사람들과 맞춰 살려고 노력하는 건 신물이 나.

Husband: 그래? 진작 그렇게 말해 주지! 훨씬 더 편하게 살았을 텐데.

Dialogue 2

Wife: 좋아, 가정 회계를 살펴 보자.

Husband: 그러면 우리가 무엇을 가지고 있지?

Wife: 대출을 받았기 때문에 전체적으로는 적자야.

Husband: 그래, 나도 기억하고 있어. 수중에 가지고 있는 돈으로 시작하자, 어때?

Wife: 은행에 현금이 좀 있어.

Husband: 여보, 은행에 있는 것이면 현금이 아니잖아.

Wife: 여기 까다롭게 구는 사람이 있네!

Dialogue 3

Husband: 대차 대조표를 만들자.

Wife: 대차 대조표? 약간 오버하는 것 아냐?

Husband: 그러면 무엇을 제안하려고?

Wife: 음, 내 급여로 기본적인 경비는 충당이 되겠지만, 휴가를 가거나 주택을 보수할 만한 여유는 없어.

Husband: 오 제발. 우리는 지난 두 달 동안 저축을 했잖아. 확실히 그중 하나에는 돈을 쓸 수 있을 거야.

Wife: 내가 선택을 해야 한다면, 아직 이러한 생각에 확신이 드는 건 아니지만, 휴가를 택하고 싶어.

Husband: 우리는 열심히 일했잖아. 휴가를 즐길 자격이 있어 – 그리고 더 나아가서 그럴 필요도 있고.

Wife: 당신 말이 맞아. 휴가 없이도 지낼 수는 있겠지만 아이들에게 어딘가로 가지고 약속을 했었어.

Husband: 그리고 그것이 휴가를 찬성해야 하는 가장 강력한 논거가 되지, 맞아.

Dialogue 4

Wife: 돈에 대해 걱정하는 거야, 아니면 일자리에 대해 걱정하는 거야?

Husband: 음, 두 개가 서로 연관된 것 아닌가, 그렇지 않아?

Wife: 내 질문에 답하지 않았어.

Husband: 돈이지.

Wife: 나 또한 가계에 기여를 하고 있다는 점을 명심해 줘.

Husband: 물론 기여하고 있지. 하지만 당신 월급만으로는 수지 균형을 맞출 수 없을 거야.

Scene 7 (55)

Film dialogue and vocabulary   p. 60~63

D: 이 집에 무단침입하는 거 안 내켜!

A: 그러시겠지! 여러분! 계획이 변경됐다! 당장 철수하고, 수색 영장 가지고 돌아온다, 알겠나?

A: 술꾼에 대한 동정심이라고는 없군, 안 그래? 어린 시절 트라우마인가?

AA: 난 할 얘기 없어. 내가 아직 살아있는 유일한 이유는 입을 다물었기 때문이라고!

A: 마실 술이 있을 때만 입을 열 거야!

D: 로버트 머리가 왜 1만 파운드를 준 거죠?

D: 좋아요! 선택의 여지가 없네요!

AA: 그만해! 다 말할게. 한 병이라도 남겨줘, 제발!

AA: 당시 내가 쪼들리는 걸 머리가 알았어. 양육비 주고 술 마시느라… 사고로 꾸며서 보험금을 타낼 계획이라고 하더군. 자기 차라며 날 안심시켰어. 그 차를 모는 것도 봤거든. 그래서 생각했지, 뭐 어때! 알아서 하겠지. 그래서 내가 브레이크를 약간 손봤어. 그 사람들을 죽일 계획인 건 나도 몰랐다고!

D: 누굴 죽여요?

AA: 캠벨 부부! 올드 베리의 부자들 말이야!

A: 자기 장인, 장모를 죽이라고 시킨 거군요?

AA: 내가 죽인 게 아니야! 난 그냥… 그 인간 말을 들은 게 너무 후회스러워! 그 뒤에 아무 말 말라고 경고하더군! 그래서 안 했지! 27년 동안이나! …이제 술 마셔도 되겠나?

Communication situations　p. 66~67

Woman: 안녕, 늦어서 미안. 내가 너무 오래 기다리게 한 것은 아니었으면 좋겠다. 무엇을 읽고 있니?

Dialogue 1

Man: 안녕, 별일 없지? 나는 내 프로젝트에 관한 작업을 하고 있어.

Woman: 아, 그 신비에 싸인 프로젝트. 언제 공개를 할 생각이야?

Man: 지금이 어떨까? 나는 시의원 선거의 후보로 나설 거야.

Woman: 정말? 무슨 말을 해야 할지 모르겠는걸.

Man: 음, 우선, 내 편에 서겠다고 제안할 수 있지.

Woman: 그렇게, 물론 그럴 거야. 하지만 왜니? 내 말은, 무엇 때문에 그러한 길을 생각하게 된 거야?

Man: 이제 내 생각을 숨김없이 표현하고 싶어.

Woman: 무슨 뜻이니?

Man: 나는 마을 사람들을 위해 무료 보육과 노인 복지를 제공할 거야.

Woman: 그리고 전 세계의 기아 문제를 해결하겠지, 네가 그 자리에 있는 동안에 말이야.

Man: 뭐라고?

Woman: 미안, 기분 상하게 할 의도는 아니었어. 하지만 그런 선거 공약을 지킨다는 건 불가능할지도 몰라.

Dialogue 2

Man: 안녕, 만나서 반가워. 나는 소셜 웹사이트들 중 한 곳의 규정을 분석하고 있는 중이었어.

Woman: 왜? 변호사들이 작성한 규칙 같은 것 말이야? 아무도 안 읽잖아.

Man: 그게 요점이야. 사람들은 자신이 동의하는 규칙에 대해 제대로 알지 못하지.

Woman: 너는 왜 항상 다른 사람들을 구제하려고 하니? 그건 그들의 문제야, 그렇지 않아?

Man: 내 아이들이 소셜 네트워크를 이용한다면 내 문제가 되지.

Woman: 인터넷에 접속하기에는 너무 어린 것 아니니? 내 말은, 계정을 만드는 일 등에 있어서.

Man: 그런 시스템이 정말로 누군가의 나이를 확인할 수 있을까?

Woman: 안전 장치들이 마련되어 있을 거야. 적어도 내가 생각하기에는 있을 것 같아.

Dialogue 3

Man: 협회나 재단을 만드는 것에 대해 생각하고 있었어, 그게 다야.

Woman: 아직 단체의 법적 지위는 결정하지 못했구나?

Man: 맞아, 아직이야.

Woman: 그래, 아직은 시간이 있다고 생각해. 무엇에 관한 것이 될 건데?

Man: 이 마을에는 정기적인 이벤트가 필요해. 그래서 나를 도와 이벤트를 기획하는 데 관심이 있는 사람들을 찾아야 해.

Woman: 그러면 아마 이벤트 단체의 설립을 고려해야 할 거야, 재단이 아니라. 최소한 재단에는 자금이 있어야 하니까.

Scene 8 (56)

Film dialogue and vocabulary   p. 70~72

G: 아! 그래… 그 경찰관을 미행하면서 보고해! 녀석들 소굴에서 만나자고!

Y: 보스, 저희가 애덤스 먼저 없앨까요? 여자와 나머지도 처리하기 전에요?

G: 아니! 아직은 안 돼!

Y: 하지만 시한폭탄 같은 놈이라고 머리가 난리 쳤잖아요!

G: 이봐, 친구들. 난 그 남자 말을 믿기가 점점 더 꺼려져. 자기가 여우처럼 약은 줄 알지만 사실은 아니거든! 그 친구 감이 점점 떨어지는 게 본능적으로 느껴져. 내가 보기엔 우리의 장기간 협력 관계를 종료해야 할 것 같아.

V: 복잡한 말이네요! 그 영국인 변호사를 죽여요? 말아요?

G: 죽일지도 모르지, 블라드. 유리, 운전해!

O: 응?

A: 그 디스크에 시간 낭비 그만해!

A: 알아낸 게 있어! 잘 들어! 머리가 애덤스를 시켜서 장인, 장모를 살해했어.

O: 알았어… 나한테 좋은 수가 있어. 와서 얘기해.

B: 여보세요

O: 올리브 그린이에요. 기억나세요?

B: 어떻게 잊겠어요? 내 아들과 남편을 바보로 만든 영리한 아가씨였죠. 나한테 원하는 게 뭐죠?

ask for help

O: 남편을 처리하기 위해 부인의 도움이 필요해요.

B: 미안해요. 로버트를 배신하면 안 된다는 걸 오래전에 배웠어요. 혼자서 잘 해봐요, 올리브. 하지만 행운을 빌어요!

make a proposal

O: 부인의 인생을 바꿀 수 있는 멋진 제안이 있어요!

B: 그래요? 그렇다면 말해봐요. 난 새 출발을 할 준비가 됐거든요.

Communication situations   p. 74~75

Investor: 프레젠테이션을 시작하기에 앞서, 당신 업체는 우리가 신뢰성과 재정적인 전망 차원에서 평가를 하게 될 다섯 곳의 신규 기업 중 하나라는 점을 기억해 주세요. 자, 이제 당신 차례입니다.

Dialogue 1

Entrepreneur: 고맙습니다. 신사 숙녀 여러분, 저는 프레젠테이션을 시작하지 않을 것입니다.

Investor: 안 한다고요?

Entrepreneur: 그렇습니다. 여러분들께서 제 질문에 답을 해 주셨으면 좋겠습니다.

Investor: 흥미로운 접근법이군요. 질문이 무엇이죠?

Entrepreneur: 필요하지 않은 것이 무엇인가요?

Investor: 제게 개인적으로 묻는 건가요, 아니면 다른 심사위원들에게 묻는 건가요?

Entrepreneur: 바로 그것입니다. 여러분 각자가 서로 다른 대답을 할 것이니까요.

Investor: 음, 그런 아이디어는 그다지 혁신적이지 않군요. 요점이 무엇인가요?

Entrepreneur: 트렌드는 잊고 독창적인 생각을 하는 것입니다.

Investor: 실망시키고 싶지는 않지만 다른 프레젠테이션에서도 매번 비슷한 말을 듣고 있어요. 당신 아이디어는 다른 사람들의 아이디어와 어떻게 다른가요?

Entrepreneur: 안정적인 라이프스타일을 추구하는 사람을 위한 맞춤형 쇼핑이죠.

Investor: 좋습니다. 당신은 흥미로운 후보지만 저희에게 보다 자세한 내용을 알려 주어야 해요. 수요일에 다시 오세요.

Dialogue 2

Entrepreneur: 먼저, 2차 심사에 초대해 주셔서 모든 분께 감사를 드립니다.

Investor: 음, 당신은 우리의 호기심을 자극했어요. 이번에는 어떻게 하는지 봅시다.

Entrepreneur: 그런 말씀을 들으니 기쁘군요. 그러면 시작하겠습니다.

Investor: 네, 그래요. 그러죠. 재정. 자금. 그리고 큰 문제인데 – 어떻게 조달할 거죠?

Entrepreneur: 저희 신생 업체의 성장을 위한 첫 번째 단계에서는 유럽 연합의 보조금과 정부 보조금의 지원을 받았습니다.

Investor: 잘 하셨군요. 자금을 마련할 수 있는 훌륭한 재원이죠. 자, 저희에게서 무엇을 바라시나요?

Entrepreneur: 저는 대량 생산을 시작하려고 하는데 가동 첫 해에 대한 자본이 필요합니다.

Investor: 상당히 특이하군요. 첫 해가 끝나면 자기 자본 수익률이 얼마가 될 것으로 예상하시나요?

Entrepreneur: 첫 해 이후 현실적인 시나리오에서는 약 15%입니다.

Investor: 네, 합리적인 추정치군요. 자, 그 후 3년에서 5년까지의 성장률 예측에 관한 이야기를 해 봅시다.

Dialogue 3

Entrepreneur: 요점이 무엇이죠? 당신은 제가 원하는 돈이 얼마인지에 주된 관심이 있으시잖아요. 제 프로젝트가 아니라요.

Investor: 음, '젊은 기업인 프로그램'의 규정에 따르면 저희는 저희가 지원하는 사업에 대해 알아야 해요. 하지만 좋아요. 솔직하게 말씀해 보세요.

Entrepreneur: 좋습니다. 제가 돈을 요구하지 않고 후원을 요구한다면 어떻게 하실 건가요?

Investor: 이봐요, 당신은 이 회의를 뒤엎고 있어요. 당신은 우리가 당신 규칙대로 움직이기를 원하는군요.

Scene 9 (57)

Film dialogue and vocabulary   p. 78~79

D: 이럴 때가 아니면, 언제 경찰을 부르겠어요! 확증도 있고 애덤스도 증언할 준비가 됐어요!

A: 맞아, 눈앞에 술병만 달랑거리면 되지!

O: 안 돼요!

D: 그럼 나더러 어쩌라고요?

O: 내가 해결할 테니까 나만 믿어요.

D: 뭐야?

A: 꽁지머리를 한 놈이 게나디 코롤료프야. 러시아 최대 마피아 조직의 영국 지부 두목이지. 그 옆이 그의 오른팔, 유리. 런던을 통틀어 가장 지독하고 악랄한 조폭 중 한 명이야! 덩치 큰 남자는… 영국 순회공연 중인 볼쇼이 발레 단원은 아닐 거야. 좋아, 알피, 생각해… 만나서 반가웠어, 데이비드. 이렇게 만나지 않았다면 아주 친한 친구가 됐을 텐데! 올리브, 나의 올리브! 내 평생의 사랑이 될 수도 있었지만, 지금은 살기 위해 이기적일 필요가 있을 거 같아! 난 죽을 필요가 없는데, 같이 몰살되는 건 이상하잖아. 그럼, 잘 해봐!

O: 데이비드, 안 돼요! 날 믿어요. 내가 해결할 수 있어요! 내가 얘기해 볼게요!

D: 좋아요, 올리브. 당신이 맡아요! (…) 다음 기회가 없을지도 모르니까요!

G: 이런, 어디부터 시작하지?

Communication situations   p. 84~85

Clerk: 안녕하세요, 세무서입니다. 어떻게 도와 드릴까요?

Dialogue 1

Entrepreneur: 제가 회사를 설립했는데 VAT 등록을 해야 한다고 들었어요.

Clerk: 맞습니다. 과세 매출이 81,000파운드를 넘으면 등록을 하셔야 합니다.

Entrepreneur: 하지만 이제 막 시작해서 앞으로의 매출에 대해서는 알지 못하는걸요.

Clerk: 그러시군요. 그러면 과세 분기점을 넘으실 때 등록하셔야 합니다. 81,000파운드가 되는 시점이죠. 좋은 하루 보내십시오!

Dialogue 2

Entrepreneur: 안녕하세요, 소득 신고서 제출 때문에 전화를 드렸어요. 자세한 내용이 필요해서요.

Clerk: 좋습니다. 개인 사업자신가요, 유한 회사인가요?

Entrepreneur: 개인 사업자요.

Clerk: 안타깝지만 전화로 하실 수는 없으세요. 양식을 우편으로 보내시거나 온라인 계정을 이용하셔야 해요.

Entrepreneur: 하지만 온라인 계정은 가지고 있지 않는데요.

Clerk: 그러시면 귀하의 UTR 숫자에 대해 여쭤봐야겠군요. 하지만 진행하기에 앞서, 서비스 품질과 교육 목적으로 통화가 기록될 수 있다는 점을 알려 드릴게요.

Entrepreneur: 네, 알겠어요. UTR 숫자가 무엇인가요?

Clerk: 좋습니다. 이미 '세금 자진 신고'에 등록하셨나요?

Entrepreneur: 네, 등록했고, 이틀 동안 활성화 코드를 기다리고 있는 중이에요.

Clerk: 맞습니다. 활성화 코드는 근무일 기준 7일 이내에 도착할 거예요. 하지만 등록하실 때 '고유 납세자 참조' 번호를 받으셨어야 해요.

Entrepreneur: 그렇군요. 정말 고맙습니다.

Clerk: 전화 주셔서 감사합니다.

Dialogue 3

Entrepreneur: 안녕하세요, 소득 신고서를 제출하고 싶어요.

Clerk: 안타깝지만 전화로 하실 수는 없으세요. 양식을 우편으로 보내시거나 온라인 계정을 이용하셔야 해요.

Entrepreneur: 하지만 로그인을 할 수가 없어요.

Clerk: 그러시면 귀하의 UTR 숫자에 대해 여쭤봐야겠군요. 하지만 진행하기에 앞서, 서비스 품질과 교육 목적으로 통화가 기록될 수 있다는 점을 알려 드릴게요.

Entrepreneur: 녹음은 동의할 수 없어요.

Clerk: 좋습니다. 아쉽지만, 그런 경우라면 통화를 계속할 수가 없습니다. 지역 국세청 사무소에 전화하셔서 도움을 요청해 보세요.

Scene 10 (58)

Film dialogue and vocabulary   p. 88~90

G: 그게, 너희가 죽어 마땅한 이유가 많아.

G: 대부분 일과 관련된 거지만 개인적인 부분도 있지… 넌… 넌 정말 눈엣가시였어. 내 아들 세르게이를 만났지, 안 그래? 지금 수단에 있어. 나한테 편지로 알려주더군. 자선단체를 도와서 지역 주민을 위해 우물을 팔 거라고. 그리고, 내가 저지른 모든 나쁜 짓에 대해 속죄해야 한다는 거야! 너 때문이야! 네가 스트레스를 줬던가 아니면 너한테 맞아서 정신이 나간 거지! 일과 관련해서는… 내가 믿을 만한 정보통한테 들은 건데, 네가 가지고 있는 정보가 있다더군. 소문에는, 그 정보의 성격이 내 사업의 적법성에 대한 의혹을 살 수 있는 거라던데.

O: 허튼소리!

G: 뭐?

O: 디스크에는 머리와의 동업에 대한 내용은 없어요. 당신이 우릴 죽이게 해서 위기를 모면하려고 그렇게 말한 거예요. 우리가 알아낸 걸 알고 있거든요.

Y: 뭘 알아내?

O: 머리가 장인, 장모를 죽여서 아내가 정신 쇠약에 걸렸고… 그걸 이용해서 정식으로 재산 관리를 넘겨받은 거예요.

Y: 제법이네요!

G: 사악한 자식! 그래도… 우린 안전한 거군! 좋아, 대화 즐거웠어.

G: 유리, 블라드, 죽여!

plead for mercy
O: 제발 죽이지 마세요! 대화로 해결해요!

take control
O: 다시 의자에 궁둥이 붙여요!

G: 내가 왜 그래야 하지!

O: 당신이 안전한 줄 알면 착각이에요. 전혀 아니에요. 당신의 그 소중한 회사가 망하기 직전이라고요! 하지만 그건 다 본인 탓이에요! 진작에 더 좋은 변호사를 구했어야죠!

G: 계속 말해봐…

Communication situations   p. 94~95

Councillor A: 신사 숙녀 여러분, 오늘의 다음 안건은 마을 잔디밭 공원의 기념물에 관한 것입니다. 우리 모두 찬성표를 던졌기 때문에, 이제 누구를 기념할 것인지 선택을 하도록 합시다. 15세기의 주교가 좋을까요, 혹은 2차 대전의 군인들이 좋을까요?

Dialogue 1

Councillor B: 일반적인 의견들은 군인을 선호하는 것으로 알고 있지만 저는 반대 의견을 가지고 있습니다.

Councillor A: 네? 그것이 무엇이죠?

Councillor B: 왜 우리가, 지역 사회에서, 그러한 기념물을 세워야 하나요?

Councillor A: 무슨 말씀이신가요?

Councillor B: 그와 같은 시련을 기념하는 기념물은 이미 많이 존재하잖아요.

Councillor A: 그러한 분쟁 때문에 6천만 명이 넘는 사람들이 목숨을 잃었다는 점을 상기시켜 드릴까요? 그들을 기리기 위한 기념비가 과다할 정도로 많다고 말씀하시는 건가요?

Councillor B: 사실, 그렇습니다.

Councillor A: 좋아요. 의견에 감사를 드립니다. 이제 다른 분들께서 어떤 말씀을 하시고 싶어하는지 확인해 봅시다.

Dialogue 2

Councillor B: 주교님을 기념해야 해요. 그는 우리 지역 출신 인물이고 기억될 만한 자격이 있죠.

Councillor A: 하지만, 확실한 부분만 말씀을 드리면, 젊은 여성에 대한 그의 태도는 논란을 불러 일으켰어요.
Councillor B: 감히 그런 말씀을 하시다니요! 그에게 불리한 물증은 한 건도 없었어요.
Councillor A: 600년 이상 된 교회 문서들에 의지하기는 힘들다는 점을 인정하셔야 해요.
Councillor B: 역사적인 문서에 의지하는 것은 그처럼 먼 옛날 일을 다루는 경우, 표준적인 절차예요.
Councillor A: 동의해요. 그리고 문제의 인물이 정말로 깨끗하다면야 모두 괜찮죠.
Councillor B: 역사적인 문서는 무시할 준비가 되어 있지만 역사적인 소문은 기꺼이 들으시겠다는 건가요?
Councillor A: 도덕성에 의심이 있는 인물을 기념해서는 안 된다는 점을 말씀드리고 있는 거예요.
Councillor B: 같은 말만 되풀이하시는군요.
Councillor A: 그럴 수도 있겠지만, 그래도 제 말이 맞아요. 어쨌든, 이제 반대 의견에 초점을 맞춰서 논의가 어떻게 진행되는지 봅시다, 그럴까요?

Scene 11 (59)

Film dialogue and vocabulary   p. 98~99

B: 기분이 어때요?
M: 뭐가 어떻긴 어때?
B: 공포, 불확실, 혼란…
M: 베아트리스, 하지 마!
B: 아직도 다 잘 될 거라는 희망을 품고 있다면 시간 낭비라는 걸 알아둬요. 러시아 친구들이 이미 오는 중일 거예요. 특히 아이러니한 점은 다 당신이 자초한 일이라는 거죠. 내 말은… 마틴요! 당신이 그를 죽게 한 다음에야 난 깨달았어요. 내가 당신을 얼마나 증오하는지를요!
M: 러시아인들에게 무슨 얘길 했지?
B: 러시아인들한테는 아무 말 안 했어요. 무섭거든요. 하지만 올리브는 귀담아듣더라고요. 정말 맘에 드는 사람이에요! 커티스와 잘 안 된 게 너무 아쉬워요! 내가 올리브에게 한 얘기를 올리브가 크롤로프 씨에게 그대로 전할 거예요. 그동안 당신이 어떻게 그 사람들을 위해 거래를 할 때마다 딴 주머니를 찼는지를요! 심지어 어마어마한 수수료를 받으면서도 말이에요! 그리고 그걸 증명할 충분한 자료도 넘길 거예요.
M: 어떻게 당신이 그 모든 걸 알았지?
B: 당신은 내가 옆에 있을 때도 아무 말이나 다 했고 누구나 읽을 수 있게 서류를 책상 위에 내버려 뒀죠. 그런 점이 아내가 멍청한 여편네라고 생각하는 남편을 둔 유일한 장점일 거야. (…)

`run away`
C: 아빠, 그냥 계세요! 친구들이 데리러 올 때까지 제가 같이 있어 드릴게요!

`attack Beatrice`
C: 아빠, 꿈도 꾸지 마세요! 엄마하고 얘기가 끝난 것 같네요. 이제 저랑도 얘기 좀 하시죠. 가시기 전에요.

Communication situations   p. 104~105

Student A: 안녕, 오늘 학교 생활은 어땠니? 오, 답을 듣기 전에. 지저분해서 미안, 이번 주는 내가 청소할 차례인 건 아는데… 나 대신 집안일을 해 줄 수 있니? 부탁할게.

Dialogue 1

Student B: 음, 내키지는 않지만 그러지. 네가 조만간 추가로 청소를 한 주 더 한다면야.

Student A: 그럼 된 거다! 그리고 정말 미안해. 선택의 여지가 없어, 오늘 이 일을 끝내야 하거든.

Student B: 거래는 거래야, 기억해. 무엇 때문에 그처럼 어려움을 겪고 있니?

Student A: 음, 나는 여기 서평을 하나 쓰고 있는 중이야.

Student B: 그렇군. 감수가 필요하면 나중에 내가 기꺼이 네 글을 살펴봐 줄게.

Student A: 네가? 그러면 좋지! 한 가지 문제가 해결되었군.

Dialogue 2

Student B: 지난 주에도 내가 너 대신 했잖아. 미안하지만 나 역시 해야 할 일이 좀 있어.

Student A: 음, 나는 여기 서평을 하나 쓰고 있는 중이야.

Student B: 그래, 이제 기억나는군. 문학 블로그를 위한 샘플 리뷰지, 맞지?

Student A: 바로 그거야.

Student B: 잘 할 수 있을 거야. 블로그의 황금률을 지켜야 한다는 점만 기억해.

Student A: 어떤 것 말이야?

Student B: 온라인으로 글을 읽는 것은 마치 사진을 휙휙 넘겨보는 것과 같지.

Student A: 네 말이 이해가 가지 않는 걸.

Student B: 짧은 텍스트, 간결한 단락, 그리고 재치 있는 제목이지.

Student A: 나는 지적인 리뷰를 쓰고 있어, 저질 신문의 "주의를 끄는 글"이 아니라. 네 방식은 너 자신한테 발송되는 대량 스팸 메일을 위해 아껴 둬.

Dialogue 3

Student B: 그래, 좋아. 네가 최근에 많은 일을 하는 걸 봤어. 그건 그렇고, 무엇에 관한 일을 하고 있는 거니?

Student A: 서평이야. 하지만 사실을 말하자면, 이런 종류의 저널리즘은 나와 맞지 않아.

Student B: 불평 그만하고 정면 돌파해.

Student A: 그래, 음… 이제 막 시작한 단계야. 혹은, 솔직히 말하면: 어디서부터 시작을 해야 할지 모르겠어.

Student B: 스타일에 대해 생각해 봐. 첫 문장으로 독자를 사로잡은 후, 긴장감이나 혹은 유머 감각을 계속 유지시켜.

Student A: 다 좋은 말이기는 한데, 어떻게 시작하지? 알다시피 멋진 첫 문장은 저절로 생기는 게 아니잖아.

Scene 12 (60)

Film dialogue and vocabulary p. 108~109

이성적인 인간인 게나디는 내가 베아트리스에게 들은 얘기가 그를 파멸시키기에 충분하다고 확신했다. 내가 마음먹는다면… 그래서 그는 우릴 살려줬다.

그리고 우리는 프랑스인을 풀어줬다. 클로티에는 여전히 내 "상도덕 위반"에 앙심을 품고 있었지만…

내가 알아듣게 얘기했고, 다시는 날 귀찮게 하지 않을 것이다. 소문에 따르면 그와 알피가…

미술품 사업을 함께 시작했다고 한다. 누가 상상이나 했을까?

우리는 내 상처를 치료하고 우선순위를 바로잡기 위해… 올드 베리로 돌아갔다.

난 두 달 동안 아무것도 안 훔쳤다. 그립냐고? 아니! 맞다! 가끔은!

머리는… 저택을 떠난 뒤로 묘연히 사라져버렸다.

그렇다고 그리워하는 사람은 없다. 베아트리스는 재산을 되찾았다. 커티스와 함께 잘 꾸려가고 있다.

나와 데이비드는 좋은 관계를 유지하고 있다. 사실 우리는 생각하고 있는…

여보세요? 누구세요?

Communication situations p. 112~113

Mother: 얘야, 마침내 같이 외출하게 되어서 기쁘구나. 보다 자주 이렇게 해야 하는데, 그렇게 생각하지 않니? 자, 우리가 이야기해야 할 것이 하나 있어. 네 장래 계획이 어떻게 되니?

Dialogue 1

Daughter: 저는 블로그 활동을 계속하고 싶어요.

Mother: 그래. 그에 대해 네가 정말로 큰 관심을 가지고 있다는 것은 나도 알고, 기쁘게 생각해. 하지만 나는 진지하게 묻고 있는 거야.

Daughter: 하지만 엄마, 저도 진지하게 받아들이고 있는걸요.

Mother: 네 공부는 어떻게 하고? 혹은 최소한 일은?

Daughter: 엄마, 공부는 제가 원하는 아무 때라도 시작할 수 있어요.

Mother: 그건 사실이지만, 나중에 시작할 수록 끝까지 하기가 더 어렵단다.

Daughter: 저는 동의하지 않아요, 엄마.

Mother: 동의하지 않는다고?

Daughter: 그래요, '열린 대학'이 있어요. 학사 학위도 받을 수 있고 석사 학위도 받을 수 있죠, 온라인으로요.

Mother: 정말이니? 그러면 나도 등록할 수 있겠는걸? 나는 항상 미술사를 공부해 보고 싶었거든.

Daughter: 그래요, 해 보세요, 엄마!

Mother: 고맙다, 얘야! 하지만 너에 대해서 이야기해야 하지 않을까?

Dialogue 2

Daughter: 솔직히 말씀을 드리면 저는 정체기에 빠진 것 같아요.

Mother: 왜 그렇니? 문제가 뭐니?

Daughter: 학업과 매일 반복되는 일에 지쳤어요.

Mother: 하지만 그것이 인생이란다, 얘야.

Daughter: 하지만 저는 거의 20살이고 그런 일은 하고 싶지 않아요.

Mother: 그러면 변화를 줄 수 있는 방법을 찾아야지.

Daughter: 네, 최근에 그에 대해 많이 생각해 보고 있어요.

Mother: 염두에 두고 있는 것이라도 있니?

Daughter: 여행 비용을 마련하기 위해 일을 하는 것을 생각해 보았어요.

Mother: 어디로 가고 싶은데?

Daughter: 첫 6개월 동안은 남아메리카로, 그리고 두 번째 6개월 동안은 알래스카로요.

Mother: 1년짜리 여행이로구나. 꽤 기네. 지루한 일상으로 돌아오려면 어려움을 겪게 될 수도 있어.

Dialogue 3

Mother: 오 얘야, 나는 네가 너무 많은 가십 웹사이트를 보고 있다고 생각해. 어떻게 네가 유명 인사가 될 수 있겠니?

Daughter: 정말, 소셜 미디어에 대해 모르시는군요, 그렇죠?

Mother: 그래 맞아, 잘 몰라.

Daughter: 저는 유명 인사가 되려는 것이 아니에요.

Mother: 그러면 블로그는 재미를 위해서 운영할 거니?

Daughter: 그것에 잘못된 점이라도 있나요?

Mother: 그러면 돈은 어떻게 하고?

Daughter: 저를 믿으세요, 그 비즈니스에는 많은 돈이 돌아요.

Mother: 그래, 하지만 어떻게 벌건데?

Daughter: 저를 믿으세요, 저는 소셜 미디어가 어떻게 작동하는지 잘 알아요.

Mother: 단지 너를 더 믿기만 하면 되겠구나, 그렇지? 음, 현재는 두 번 다시 오지 않는단다.